Worms, *Shadows,* *and* Whirlpools

Worms, *Shadows,* *and* Whirlpools

SCIENCE IN THE EARLY CHILDHOOD CLASSROOM

Karen Worth & **Sharon Grollman**
OF EDUCATION DEVELOPMENT CENTER, INC.

HEINEMANN
Portsmouth, NH

Newton, MA

naeyc
Washington, DC

Heinemann
A division of Reed Elsevier Inc.
361 Hanover Street
Portsmouth, NH 03801–3912
www.heinemann.com

National Association for the
Education of Young Children
1509 16th Street, N.W.
Washington, DC 20036–1426
www.naeyc.org

Offices and agents throughout the world

 This book was prepared with the support of NSF Grant ESI-9818737. However,
any opinions, findings, conclusions, and/or recommendations herein are those
of the authors and do not necessarily reflect the views of NSF.

Library of Congress Cataloging-in-Publication Data
Worth, Karen.
    Worms, shadows, and whirlpools : science in the early childhood classroom / Karen
Worth, Sharon Grollman.
        p.   cm.
    Includes bibliographical references and index.
    ISBN 0-325-00573-7
    1. Science—Study and teaching (Early childhood)—United States.   2. Science—Study
and teaching (Early childhood)—Activity programs—United States.   I. Title: Science in the
early childhood classroom.   II. Grollman, Sharon Hya.   III. Title.
LB1139.5.S35W67   2003
372.3′5—dc21   2003005885

Editor: Robin Najar
Production: Elizabeth Valway
Interior and cover design: Catherine Hawkes, Cat and Mouse
Composition: Publishers' Design and Production Services, Inc.
Manufacturing: Steve Bernier

Printed in the United States of America on acid-free paper

07   06   05   04   03   ML   1   2   3   4   5

To the many skilled and dedicated early childhood teachers
who have informed our work so deeply.

CONTENTS

Imagine a circle of preschool children, huddled near the ground, each using a Popsicle® stick to gently hold a worm. The children have found the worms in various locations of their schoolyard. Peering through hand lenses to permit close examination, the children are discussing the worms' similarities and differences.

Imagine the teacher of these children, huddled with the group, taking note of their observations. Every so often, she asks a simple question, one that prompts them to take their thinking a step further than it might go on its own. "Where did you find this?" she asks. "What do you see?"

Weeks later, after digging for more worms, discovering patterns in their locations, and making written and drawn records of their findings, the teacher and children make plans to bring the worms indoors so that they can continue their investigation. The children will go on to figure out what worms need to live, build terraria for them, systematically analyze their behaviors, and eventually set them free.

These children and this teacher see themselves as *naturalists*, special kinds of scientists who investigate living things. To learn about the world, they engage in actual scientific processes. Rather than the teacher deciding what the children should discover and providing explanations for concepts, she guides them toward articulating their own questions and observing phenomena for themselves.

That's the kind of learning environment this book will help you to create. In this book you will read about the work of this teacher and many others who have created science programs that are based on current knowledge about the ways in which young children think and learn. We know that children develop science knowledge as they observe and act on the world, asking questions, making predictions, testing those predictions, and reflecting on their experiences. Learning happens as they construct continually more sophisticated theories of how the world works. The children in this book are doing just that—through real-life science experiences.

You will read stories of children observing the development of an animal through metamorphosis; documenting the seasonal changes of a tree; exploring the science of water, blocks, and shadows; and doing much, much more. All the while, they are asking questions, making predictions, and making new discoveries. You will read the stories of their teachers as they sensitively and knowledgeably support the children's development of scientific concepts and processes. Along with the stories and descriptions, you will find helpful interpretations of what is happening and ideas that will help you to expand the thinking and planning you do for your own science instruction.

What I love about this book is that it shows that children need not wait until they are in kindergarten or third grade or high school to enjoy and *really* learn science. The children in this book are immersed in scientific activity that shows value for who they are and what they are capable of learning today. Their teachers have created intellectually responsible programs in which children smartly venture forth into the world of science with a sense of wonder and exploration.

There's something powerful about that sense of wonder and exploration. It is the impetus for many thrilling discoveries at the preschool level and has been the impetus for many thrilling discoveries—for people of all ages—throughout history. It is what has taken humankind to the inside of a cell, the depths of the Atlantic, the summit of Everest, the moon; it is what has taken us to the deeper, the higher, the more complex regions of understanding. And the limits of those understandings will continue to expand because the children of today will stretch them. Today's children are the ones who will design the first manned spacecraft to Mars, rescue the rain forests, find a cure for arthritis, and discover a diet with long-term results. This book will help you and your students to be a part of those stories, whether as knowledgeable observers, contributors, or consumers. Read it and just imagine the discoveries yet to come.

Gretchen Owocki

In writing this book, we relied on the vision and contributions of many people. First, we wish to thank the project staff of the Tool Kit for Early Childhood Science Education, housed at Education Development Center, Inc., and supported by the National Science Foundation. Staff includes: Ingrid Chalufour, Robin Moriarty, Jeffrey Winokur, Erica Fields, Kerry Ouellet, Susan Weinberg, and Martha Davis. Not only did they help us with the conceptualization of this book, they also critically reviewed many drafts and provided important support throughout the entire development process.

Since the inception of this project, we have also worked closely with a committed group of early childhood teachers: Diana Barron, Liana Bond, Cindy Hoisington, Karen Hoppe, and Terry Küchenmeister. All of these talented teachers opened up their classrooms to us and shared their thinking and their children's work. Their stories, which appear throughout the book, provide insights into best practice, while demonstrating what young children can do and learn when skillful teachers make science a major focus of the curriculum.

We also wish to thank members of our national advisory board for their guidance about the science concepts and ideas that should inform the development of science curriculum for young children: Marilou Hyson, Jeane Joyner, Lisa Nyberg, Sandy Putnam-Franklin, Jo Ellen Roseman, Jean Simpson, and Jan Tuomi. And we extend our heartfelt thanks to our reviewers: Mary Eisenberg, Ben Mardell, and Martha Davis.

And finally, we wish to acknowledge the support from the National Science Foundation, which made this effort possible.

For several weeks, the children explored the science of water: how it flows, how to make it go in different ways (even up), and how to control it. They made whirlpools, used tubes to make water pathways, and experimented with funnels. Colin was particularly fascinated by the effect of the funnels when he pushed them straight down, large end first, into the water as if they were dinosaur feet walking through water. He noticed that when he pulled them out, "they kind of stuck." When I asked why that might have happened, Pilar suggested, "Maybe it's because there is a little part that sticks out a little further and it gets caught." Another child tried it and noticed that air came out of the small hole when he pushed the funnel down. He was excited then, saying, "Feel it, feel the air. You gotta feel the air." I asked why they thought that might happen. When they couldn't answer, we checked to see if there was any water inside of the funnel when it was under water, and there was.

—Excerpt from Ms. Diego's Story

It wasn't until I became excited about plants and we really started to look at them over time that kids became interested. I decided to approach the study from a number of perspectives. This year we would study plants outside the classroom and follow a tree very closely, we would grow plants in the classroom, and we would go on a number of field trips. I really wanted the children to become aware of the plant life around them, in all its diversity, and how it changed over time. We began our tree study three weeks after school began. We went outside once a week to look at the big maple in the playground. We watched the leaves change from green to orange and yellow. And then we watched as the leaves fell and the trees became bare. Right from the start I took photographs. Each week, I took one picture of the tree from the same place and one picture of the lowest branch that the kids said looked like the letter *U*. These were mounted in order on a documentation panel with the date and a few of the children's words about how the tree and branch had changed. I eventually had a fall panel, a winter panel, and a spring panel. The children looked at these a lot and we checked them before we went outside for our tree observation to remind ourselves of what we had seen and noticed before. And when we went out, sometimes with photographs in hand (thanks to my digital camera!), we compared how the tree had changed from one time to the next. The documentation was proof that changes were happening, changes that weren't evident on a day-to-day basis.

—Excerpts from Miss Scott's Story

Why Science for Young Children?

These vignettes are drawn from stories of two teachers whose work is highlighted in this book. In the first vignette, five-year-old children puzzled over intriguing events they had discovered. Guided by their teacher's simple questions while observing closely and interacting with one another, they came up with new ideas about the relationship between air and water. In the second, Miss Scott used ongoing observation and photographic documentation to guide three- and four-year-olds in thinking about seasonal change over time. Both these teachers brought exciting inquiry-based science into their early childhood classrooms, making it a major focus of their work with children. This book aims to answer the following questions:

■ Why is science important for young children?

■ What is appropriate content for three- to five-year-olds?

■ What are the principles of a good science program?

■ How do teachers engage children in science inquiry?

There are many reasons for including science in the early childhood curriculum. First and foremost, young children are curious. They are constantly exploring the world around them, trying to make sense of what happens, and building theories to explain what they see. A toddler drops everything over the side of his high chair to see if it will fall and disappear each time; another plays peek-a-boo over and over again until she is no longer surprised. A four-year-old stacks blocks one on another, getting better and better at making taller and taller towers; another predicts that the seed she planted will start to grow if it gets water.

Classroom science provides the opportunity for children to extend this natural curiosity and building of theories. Children's theories, built on their limited experiences, may be reasonable but incomplete or wrong. For example, a child may suggest that the trees cause the wind. After all, trees move every time the child feels the wind, just like an electric fan moves when it creates wind. Teachers can provide children with more focused experiences to challenge their ideas and to help them develop new and more-complex theories about the things and events in the world around them. From these experiences, children can develop a greater appreciation and understanding of the natural world.

Science in the early childhood classroom also provides children with direct experience with materials, events, and ideas that are important to later learning. Theories about forces and motion can emerge from a carefully designed block area. Exploration of the outdoors and close observation of indoor organisms provide a foundation for deeper understanding of life science. Experimentation at the water table raises interesting questions about the properties and behavior of water, answers to which are fundamental to an understanding of the nature of liquids and other forms of matter.

When children engage in science exploration in the early childhood classroom, they are doing what we call *science inquiry*. They explore the materials or the event; they ask questions; they investigate; they record and represent their work; they reflect on what they have done and what it means. And they create new theories or ideas about how the world works. These skills, ways of thinking, and attitudes are important to many areas of learning throughout life.

Finally, science is important for early childhood classrooms because it encourages *all* children to engage with the content and thinking of science. With more parents working, hands-on exploration such as playing in the sink or raising a pet is less likely to occur in the home. More and more, it is in the early childhood classroom where early experience with the natural world must take place. All children need many opportunities to be curious, follow up on their curiosity, make sense of their world, and build a foundation for understanding basic science concepts.

Despite all of these compelling reasons, many people still argue that the primary goals of the early childhood curriculum are to provide early reading, mathematics, and social skill development, leaving little time for science. To this we would say that doing inquiry-based science, by its very nature, requires the use of language, mathematics, and social skills. A science program will not detract from the learning of these basic skills. Rather, a science program will provide the meaningful context in which these skills can be learned best.

About This Book

This book is for educators who work with young children. Our goal is to present and discuss what good science teaching and learning can and should be in classrooms of children ages three to five. Is it not a "how-to" book. By focusing on content and providing examples of the work of children and teachers, we hope to raise expectations of what children can do and learn when science is a major focus of the curriculum.

The book draws from many sources. The most important source is the teachers, from Head Start, kindergarten, day care, and preschool programs, who have allowed us to capture their work and the work of their children. Their knowledge, skill, and excitement have inspired and motivated us. The book also reflects the current view of science and science education that is clearly described in *National Science Education Standards* (1996), developed by the National Academy of Sciences, and *Benchmarks for Science Literacy* (1993), developed by the American Association for the Advancement of Science. Both of these documents have guided the changes in K–12 science education of the past decade. Our work also reflects current understanding about how children learn and draws heavily from the work on developmentally appropriate practice of the National Association for the Education of Young Children.

Part One of the book provides a brief overview of important characteristics of a high-quality science program for children age three to five and some of the important tasks teachers perform to make it a reality.

Part Two is about the content of science education for young children. It begins with a chapter on inquiry, describing the important skills, ways of thinking, and attitudes that are at the heart of all scientific understanding and at the core of an effective early childhood science program. The chapters that follow focus on life, physical, earth, and space sciences. Each begins with an overview of the science concepts and ideas that should guide the development of science curriculum for young children. These are followed by composite stories drawn from early childhood classrooms that illustrate critical aspects of science content and science teaching. Each story is accompanied by a commentary highlighting particular teaching strategies and child learning.

Part Three of the book includes questions that practitioners frequently ask about inquiry-based science in the early childhood classroom. We hope that the responses we provide will spark ongoing dialogue, which will lead to a deeper understanding of principles and practices essential to quality science programs.

Worms, *Shadows,* *and* Whirlpools

PART ONE

Principles and Practices
Essential to Quality
Science Programs

CHAPTER 1

The Science Program in the Early Childhood Classroom

The Science Program

High-quality science programs for children ages three through five are based on an understanding of how children learn, what they are capable of learning, and appropriate science content. In such programs, science is an integral part of the classroom, supporting and supported by the overall goals for young children. In the hands of a skilled teacher, a good science program emerges from a carefully designed environment, clear goals, and children's interests, questions, and play. Science is not confined to a science table or focused on learning facts. Nor is it found in projects that focus on a narrow topic that does not involve direct experience, such as a study of bears or penguins.

Given the importance of community and family, and the individuality of each teacher and child, there is no single best science curriculum or program, but a high-quality early childhood science program always reflects the following characteristics:

- *It builds on children's prior experiences, backgrounds, and early theories.* All children come to school with experiences and the ideas and theories they have constructed to make sense of their surroundings. Some of these early conceptions do not reflect established scientific theories. However, they may reveal a significant capacity to reason from experience and knowledge. For example, in one of the stories in this book, children study a tree. Observing the defoliated tree in the late fall sparks a classroom discussion about whether the tree is alive. While some children had not considered the tree to be

3

alive even with its leaves, most agreed that without leaves, it was certainly dead. Some of these children had likely reasoned that the living things they knew all moved, thus the tree was not alive. Others with experience with dead plants "knew" that dead trees had no green leaves, thus this tree was dead.

A study of children's early theories leads one to recognize and value how children use their experiences to create logical explanations for how the world works. A good science program provides children with opportunities to share their ideas in multiple ways through both actions and words. Rather than being designed to correct early ideas, teach information, or provide explanations, new experiences provide children with opportunities to broaden their thinking and build new understandings.

■ *It draws on children's curiosity and encourages children to pursue their own questions and develop their own ideas.* In an environment with carefully chosen materials and many opportunities to explore and ponder, children will raise many questions both in words and in actions. For example, in one of the stories in this book, the classroom terrarium filled with worms elicited a wide range of questions including, "How do worms hug? Do worms have feet? How do worms have babies? Do worms fight?" In the physical sciences, where children interact directly with materials and events and feedback is immediate, questions may focus more directly on experimentation. For example, at the water table, a child asks, "How do I get water in [this tube]?" And sometimes a child's question is in her actions. The child who carefully makes her ramp steeper before rolling her ball down may be wondering, "What will happen if I make this ramp steeper?"

In a good science program, children are encouraged to actively pursue such questions as "How do I get water in the tube?" or "What will happen if I make this ramp steeper?" Other questions that cannot be explored through close observation and simple experimentation, such as "How do worms have babies?" can be answered using books or other resources. Still others, such as "Why is the sky blue?" are best left for children's own discussions.

In good science programs, questioning, trying things out, and taking risks are expected and valued. There is a balance between children's pursuit of their own interests and ideas and the pursuit of questions and ideas generated by other children or the teacher herself.

■ *It engages children in in-depth exploration of a topic over time in a carefully prepared environment.* Time is a critical component of a good early childhood science program. When children explore a few concepts repeatedly in many different ways, they have the opportunity to think, analyze, and reflect on their work. Thus, they are able to organize what they know into deeper and more powerful theories or ideas. The teachers highlighted in this book engage their children in science studies that last for weeks, if not months. One-week projects or twenty-minute choice times simply cannot provide sufficient time for children to explore deeply.

Carefully selected materials are fundamental, creating many possibilities for children's explorations of science concepts and the development of the skills and processes of scientific inquiry. For each area of study, children need materials that they can use in multiple ways and that lead to interesting challenges and events. For example, during an exploration of water flow, children can use materials such as tubes, connectors, cups, funnels, and basters to create many ways for water to move. They also need tools such as magnifiers, measuring devices, and clipboards for observation, measurement, and the gathering and recording of data.

At the same time, materials that detract from the particular focus may need to be removed for a while. For example, removing the dolls and dishes from the water table provides space for other materials that highlight water flow. Teachers may also need to remove those items that are less open-ended. For example, a water wheel allows for only pouring water into the opening at the top to watch the wheel spin. There is little opportunity to actually control the flow of water or how it hits the wheel.

■ *It encourages children to reflect on, represent, and document their experiences and share and discuss their ideas with others.* Direct experience with materials is critical but is not enough. Children also need to reflect on their work. They need to analyze their experiences, think about ideas such as patterns and relationships, try out new theories, and communicate with others. These processes allow children to think in new ways about what they did, how they did it, and what is significant to them.

Good science programs encourage children to document and represent their work in multiple ways—through drawings, dramatization, 3-D models, and dictation. Their teachers document as well, using photographs, video, drawings, and words. They use the documentation with children to help them reflect on their work. For example, a teacher might use children's drawings to help children describe and think about the role of different parts of plants they have observed.

Good programs also encourage ongoing discussion among children, between teacher and child, and in structured small- and large-group discussions. Such science talks are key, helping children to clarify their thinking with words and use evidence to support their developing theories, while learning from the perspectives of others.

- *It is embedded in children's daily work and play and is integrated with other domains.* A good science program is skillfully integrated into the total life of the classroom. Science may be the focus for a major project, such as living things or building structures. Science work may result from answering questions or exploring interests that emerge as children are cooking, looking at a book, painting, or

Figure 1–1
*Three-Year-Old
Malek Drawing the
Tower He Just
Built*

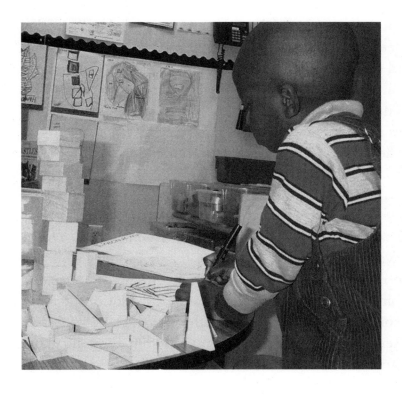

talking about something from home. Children's play also can lead them to pursue science ideas. Sailing boats at the water table can lead to exploration of what sinks and what floats. Building a cave for the classroom bear can serve as an impetus for exploring the challenges of making strong buildings and roofs that span significant distances.

Science explorations are also integrally related to other domains. Many early mathematical ideas, such as number, pattern, and shape, are part of science, as are skills of counting and early measurement. Children sort their leaves by shape, compare the length of their worms and the height of their block towers. Scientific inquiry, mathematical problem solving, and technological design all take place as children build an environment for a worm, make shadow puppets, or create drums that have different sounds.

By its very nature, science requires language, communication, and the use of books. The use of language deepens children's understanding of the science with which they are engaged. And as children collect data and represent their work, they may begin to write words, learn new vocabulary, and express themselves using many different media.

It provides access to science experiences for all children. In a good science program, teachers are aware of each child's strengths, interests, needs, and challenges. They provide many entry points into a topic and use many strategies to engage children in science explorations. For example, tabletop blocks allow the child in a wheelchair to experience the challenge of building a structure that is tall and strong. Capitalizing on a child's fascination with knights and kings can encourage him to build castles with strong fortresses. Exploring drops may be fascinating to the child who has no interest in the water table. Many teachers have found that the active and challenging nature of scientific exploration often engages children who have trouble with classroom expectations. And, because science is the exploration of real things and events, children who are learning English can become fully engaged, while demonstrating what they know and can do.

At the core of this book is a belief that the rich experiential environment of a good science program for young children provides opportunities for all children to deepen their understanding of science ideas. It lays the foundation for meeting a fundamental goal of education, which is expressed in *National Science Education Standards:* "All students, regardless of age, sex, culture or ethnic background, disabilities, aspirations or interest and motivation in science should have the opportunity to attain high levels of scientific literacy" (National Research Council 1996, 20).

The Teacher

Implementing a high-quality early childhood science program builds on what many teachers in early childhood classrooms are already doing as they provide opportunities for children's learning. At the same time, a science program builds on what children are already doing as they play outside, build with blocks, mix paints at the easel, and feed the guinea pig. But as you will see in the chapters that follow, teaching science also means making science the focus of children's work. Creating and maintaining such a focus requires that teachers take on some new tasks and become inquirers about science and about teaching science to young children. How teachers do this depends on the teacher, the children, the science focus, and the larger community. But what they do is the same for all.

- *They choose a focus for inquiry.* The first step is to think about which science ideas or concepts will be the topic for children's inquiry. They may come from a particular interest expressed by a group of children. Perhaps children have shown an interest in the bugs and worms they have found outside, so the topic becomes the needs of living things and how they are met. Or maybe the children have been racing their cars down ramps in the block area, and thus the topic would be how things move. Some new musical instruments in the classroom might suggest a focus on different sounds and what makes them. Or the teacher may choose a topic she feels is important for the children to explore but which they have not come up with themselves. Some questions a teacher might ask as she makes her decision include:

  - Is this topic interesting and engaging to my children?

  - Does the topic draw from and connect to their experience?

- Can the children explore the topic directly over time through hands-on activity?

- What are the basic science concepts for children to think about?

- Are the concepts ones my age group can handle?

- *They prepare themselves to teach the topic.* Many teachers do not have a strong background in science and need to spend time preparing to teach it. Reading books, exploring the Web, and talking with others are all good strategies to acquire some background knowledge and clarify a set of specific goals for a topic. Perhaps most important, however, is working directly with the materials the children will use. By playing, inquiring, and experimenting, teachers can find out what the materials do. They can anticipate some of the things children might do or ask, think of a challenge or focus that might lead to interesting ideas, and be prepared to engage in interesting discussion with children about their work.

- *They create a physical environment that supports inquiry.* Hands-on exploration is at the heart of inquiry. Therefore, teachers need to think about making adequate spaces for this work, selecting materials that will encourage children to explore, and often deciding which materials need to be removed temporarily to encourage in-depth science investigations. Regardless of the focus, teachers might ask themselves the following questions.

  - Is the area large enough for several groups of children to work together? Are there additional places to work on these ideas?

  - What materials will focus children's attention on the science ideas?

  - What materials should I add?

  - What materials can I remove?

  - Are materials such as markers, paper, and clipboards, which children can use to document and represent their work, accessible?

  - What books and pictures can I display to encourage children's science explorations?

- *They plan a schedule that allows time for inquiry.* Children need time to explore a topic in depth. Many explorations can last for weeks, if not months. Building time into the daily schedule is critical; choice times of forty-five minutes to an hour allow children to explore new concepts and ideas more deeply. A regular discussion time after choice time or at the end of the day helps children share experiences and their ideas. Teachers might look at their schedules and ask:

- Is the choice/activity time long enough for children's explorations?

- Do I have enough whole-group time to discuss what children are doing and thinking?

- Can my class devote several weeks or more on this topic? If so, how can I arrange my classroom schedule?

- *They foster children's questioning.* Children raise many questions as they engage with science exploration. As teachers listen to children's questions they need to ask themselves:

  - Can this question be explored directly? If so, can I provide the support and materials children need to continue?

  - Can this question be rephrased so that it can be explored directly? (For example, "Why doesn't the water come out of the baster?" can be rephrased as "How do you think we can get the water to come out of the baster?")

  - Does this question need to be answered by using resources, such as a book, the Web, or an expert? If so, what resource would be best?

  - Is this question for discussion only?

  Even if it is not possible to follow up on every question and every idea, teachers can use a variety of strategies to let children know their ideas are valued and respected. For example, teachers can save questions on charts, discuss interesting ideas, and where possible help individual children follow up on a new idea or question.

- *They encourage children's work and deepen their understanding.* Teachers need to encourage children to pursue their ideas and questions through various means. They may spend time with children to show how much the children's work is valued. They may add materials to support children's work and suggest ways to collaborate with others. But teachers also need to go further, encouraging and challenging children to think about their experiences. They need to ask about what happened, why children think it happened, and what they might do next. They need to discuss predictions of what might happen and what theories they have about the particular phenomenon/materials.

Strategies teachers can use to deepen children's understanding include the following:

■ *Engage children in conversation as they work.* Using words to describe their observations and ideas can help children think more deeply about their work. Sometimes children talk with one another quite spontaneously. Other times, teachers engage with them when children are ready to talk. Observing carefully is the first step in deciding whether or not to interact. If children are working intently, they may not want or need to be interrupted. Observation also provides the teacher with insights about what question or challenge a child might be working on and guides her in how to engage. Is it how to build a high tower or keep the dinosaur from escaping? Might it be how to create a drinking

Figure 1–2
A Teacher Supporting Children's Building Explorations

fountain or figure out how the worm eats? Descriptive questions are good to start with: "Can you tell me what you have done?" "What was hard about this work?" Other kinds of questions and new materials challenge children to go further: "Could you use these smaller blocks to make your tower even taller? What is important to keep your tower from falling down?" "The dinosaur is strong. What could you do to make the wall stronger?" "How do you know that the worm eats dirt? How could we find out if it likes other things?"

■ *Lead group discussions.* Small- and whole-group science talks where children discuss their experiences and their thinking lead children to think in new and deeper ways about science. If teachers take brief notes as children work, they will have many starting points for these discussions. Children's representations, photographs, documentation panels, and the materials themselves can also deepen the discussion. "Alonzo, tell us about how you made the walls for your dinosaur house very strong." "Alicia, can you explain this picture you made of your building? How many blocks did you use for the tower part?" "Mira, show us how you made the shadow that looked like a frog." As children share their work, teachers also help them make connections between what they have been doing, what others have been doing, and what they already know. "What materials do we need to make a home for our worms? When we were outside, what did we find out they need?" "What was something a lot of you did to make your ball go down the ramp faster?"

■ *Encourage children to document and represent their work.* When children document and/or represent their work, they think about their experiences in new ways. Drawing a picture in his naturalist's notebook of a worm will often prompt a child to observe more closely and highlight details. The challenge of painting flowing water may enhance a child's sense of the continuity of the flow of water. Encouraging children to represent involves making materials, such as clipboards, different papers, and collage materials, accessible as children explore. It also means working closely with children, prompting them to look again, to be sure of the color they are using, to count the blocks in the tall tower once more. And it means celebrating what gets done.

■ *Document what is happening.* Documenting the science work in the classroom—using words, video, photographs, and children's work—can help children see what happens over time and revisit an event that happens very quickly. The plant gets bigger and bigger; the caterpillar changes into a butterfly. Pictures of children's work over time can also make the process of inquiry visible, such as showing the steps in making a musical instrument or in constructing a system of tubes and funnels to empty the water table into the sink. This documentation then provides a focus for conversations among children, and among children and adults. Making a documentation panel that tells a story with pictures and words is a particular way to give children a chance to see the "story" of their work laid out for them.

■ *They observe and assess individual children and the group.* Ongoing observation and assessment is a critical part of teaching science in the early childhood classroom. Teachers need to know about children's experiences, the play they invent, and what interests them and what does not. They also need to try to understand the possible meanings behind their questions, the theories they are working on, and how they communicate their ideas.

To do this, teachers must become observers and recorders of what is happening as children explore. They may take notes on individual children or groups. They may keep checklists of who has worked where, take pictures, make documentation panels, and keep samples of children's work. While taking the time to observe can be a challenge with all of the day-to-day demands, the data teachers collect is invaluable in a number of ways. Data can help teachers make decisions about the curriculum, what the group will do next, and the types of adaptations needed for individual children. The data can also serve as a springboard for talking with caretakers and staff about the progress of individual children and the purpose and value of the children's science experiences.

As they think about observing and assessing children, teachers might ask:

■ Do I have a clear set of goals and expectations for science?

■ Do I have a plan so that my assessment is systematic?

- What different assessment strategies will I use?

- How will I keep records of children's experiences and what they are thinking and learning?

Summing Up

Characteristics of a high-quality science program:

- It builds on children's prior experiences, backgrounds, and early theories.

- It draws on children's curiosity and encourages children to pursue their own questions and develop their own ideas.

- It engages children in in-depth exploration of a topic over time in a carefully prepared environment.

- It encourages children to reflect on, represent, and document their experiences and share and discuss their ideas with others.

- It is embedded in children's daily work and play and is integrated with other domains.

- It provides access to science experiences for all children.

The tasks teachers do:

- They choose a focus for inquiry.

- They prepare themselves to teach a topic.

- They create a physical environment that supports inquiry.

- They plan a schedule that allows time for inquiry.

- They foster children's questioning.

- They encourage children's work and deepen their understanding.

- They observe and assess individual children and the group.

PART TWO

The Science Content

Part Two of this book is about the "what" of the early childhood science program. Because doing and learning about inquiry are critical content areas of science, we start with a description of inquiry. The chapters that follow focus on areas of science, or subject matter, that can provide the most meaningful experiences for children ages three to five. We describe a set of core ideas in life, physical, and earth and space sciences that young children can explore and how these ideas can become central to classroom work.

The particular ideas of life science, physical science, and earth and space science have been selected because all are intrinsically interesting to many children and likely to spark their curiosity. They are about concepts that young children can explore directly as they make sense of the world around them and everyday events in their lives. Moreover, current educational research suggests they are within the grasp of children ages three through five. And finally, they correspond to the concepts and ideas of science detailed in *National Science Education Standards* (National Research Council 1996) and *Benchmarks for Science Literacy* (American

Association for the Advancement of Science 1993) that children will learn in greater depth and more formally as they move through school.

Each of the subject-matter chapters includes classroom stories that illustrate the science of the classroom and how children's use of the inquiry processes is as the heart of their science learning.

CHAPTER 2

Inquiry in the Early Childhood Classroom

Science inquiry refers to the diverse ways in which scientists study the natural world and propose explanations based on the evidence derived from their work. Inquiry also refers to the activities of students in which they develop knowledge and understanding of scientific ideas, as well as an understanding of how scientists study the natural world.

—National Research Council 1996, 23

Skills of Inquiry

It is not surprising that many have called children "natural scientists." Young children are curious and intent on making sense of their physical and social environment. Enthusiastic explorers of materials, organisms, and events, they bring to their work and play a sense of wonder and a natural desire to inquire. But curiosity alone is not enough for children to develop skills and promote their understanding. For children to develop the skills of scientific inquiry, adult guidance is essential. Teachers can foster such inquiry by building on children's spontaneous exploration and gradually guiding them to become more focused and systematic in their observations and investigations.

Developing children's inquiry skills is a fundamental goal of an early childhood science program. Children need many opportunities to develop and use these skills. But these skills should not be taught in isolation from interesting topics and ideas and children's ongoing play. Rather, children need to develop their abilities to use inquiry in the context of their experiences with interesting materials and meaningful science ideas. Some specific skills, such as using a magnifier or measuring an object, may require direct instruction. Other skills, such as sorting and categorizing, may also be reinforced or practiced using games or simple activities. But mostly, children will use these skills in a context in which they matter.

There are many different skills that make up scientific inquiry. They include children's ability to:

- raise questions about objects and events around them

- explore objects, materials, and events by acting upon them and noticing what happens

- make careful observation of objects, organisms, and events using all of their senses

- describe, compare, sort, classify, and order in terms of observable characteristics and properties

- use a variety of simple tools to extend their observations (e.g., hand lenses, measuring tools, eyedroppers, a balance)

- engage in simple investigations including making predictions, gathering and interpreting data, recognizing simple patterns, and drawing conclusions

- record observations, explanations, and ideas through multiple forms of representation including drawings, simple graphs, writing, and movement

- work collaboratively with others

- share and discuss ideas and listen to new perspectives

It can be helpful to think about children's inquiry in the classroom as a process that often proceeds through several stages. In each stage, certain inquiry skills are emphasized. The framework for Young Children's Inquiry (see Figure 2–1) suggests that the stages follow one another. To some extent they do, but as the many arrows suggest, the process of inquiry is not linear; children, just as scientists do, will move back and forth and around as they explore.

In the first stage, children notice and wonder as they freely explore materials with little direct guidance. As children explore, many will ask a lot of questions. Others may not put these questions into words, but will act on them. The child who carefully chooses a block and places it on her tower is "asking" something about how to make tall or strong towers. As work continues, some children may be struck by a particular

Figure 2–1

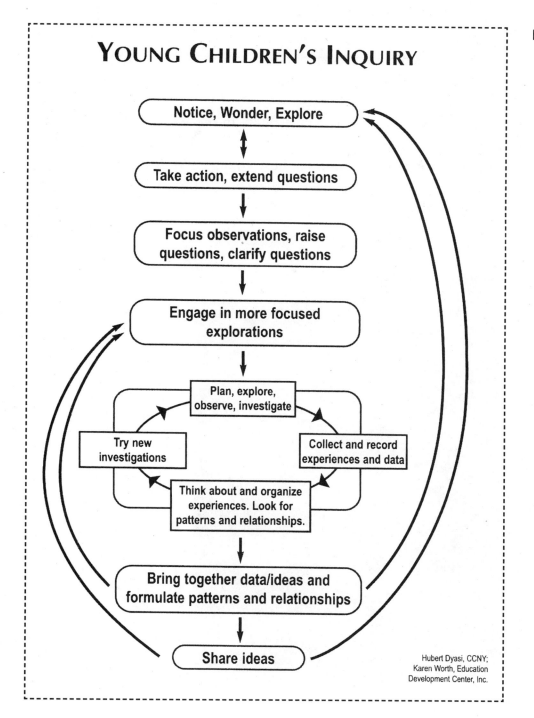

YOUNG CHILDREN'S INQUIRY

Notice, Wonder, Explore

Take action, extend questions

Focus observations, raise questions, clarify questions

Engage in more focused explorations

Plan, explore, observe, investigate

Try new investigations

Collect and record experiences and data

Think about and organize experiences. Look for patterns and relationships.

Bring together data/ideas and formulate patterns and relationships

Share ideas

Hubert Dyasi, CCNY;
Karen Worth, Education
Development Center, Inc.

idea or question, such as "How high can we make our building before it falls?" Rather than answering children's questions directly, teachers can provide the encouragement and support that children need to follow up.

Children often need adult guidance to move to the second stage, where they focus their observations and raise questions that can be investigated. "Where do the worms come from?" is not one they can explore directly, but "What are the kinds of places in our yard the worms seem to want to be?" can be pursued. Similarly, "Why does the water go down?" demands an explanation, whereas "What are ways I can get the water to go from this container to that one?" provides a springboard for an investigation.

As children explore and investigate in more focused explorations, they are likely to use many of the skills of inquiry. In the classroom stories, there are many examples of how young children plan, explore, observe, and investigate; collect and record data; represent their ideas; think about and organize experiences; look for patterns and relation-

Figure 2–2 *"How high can we make our building before it falls?"*

ships; and try new investigations. Notice that the process is cyclical. Children may explore a question for a long time, and their explorations may lead to new questions and new investigations. For example, observing snails may prompt an exploration of how they move and how they eat.

New ideas in science are built on the experiences and ideas of others. In the final stage of this framework, teachers bring children to share and discuss their conclusions and formulate ideas and theories.

Attitudes of Inquiry

Doing science builds children's inquiry skills; it also fosters a set of attitudes that are important to science and other areas as well. Scientific inquiry is not a dry process or method. Instead, true scientific inquiry is imbued with excitement, creativity, and wonder—fostering children's appreciation of the world they live in, both its beauty and its complexities. At the same time, it encourages children to take risks and pursue new challenges.

Perhaps the most important attitude to maintain is curiosity. Teachers can build on and nurture children's curiosity by making the classroom studies interesting and responsive to their questions. It also is important to encourage questioning that takes children more deeply into their explorations. Connected to curiosity is the willingness to try something out and keep at it. Children often need help as they pursue their questions or new challenges, but by not jumping in too soon, teachers can encourage children to work through their frustrations and feel the satisfaction of accomplishment.

Critical to science is a respect for evidence. Teachers and children should frequently ask questions such as "Why do you think so?" "What did you do?" and "What did you observe?" Records of data and representations of work should be part of sharing as often as possible. A debate about results, such as whose truck went the farthest, should be resolved by doing it again.

And science is a collaborative endeavor. Scientists often work in groups; similarly, group work is the norm in the classroom stories. Constructing new ideas is also a collaborative effort. Carefully guided discussions of work done, new ideas, and differences can help children develop an appreciation of the work of others and a willingness to discuss and debate findings.

The classroom stories included in the following chapters are filled with examples of children inquiring and developing their abilities to explore a question or event or object. They also illustrate the many strategies that teachers can use to support and facilitate the work children are doing.

Figure 2–3 *A Documentation Panel That a Teacher Made After Her Class of Three- to Five-Year-Old Children Studied Snails for Several Weeks*

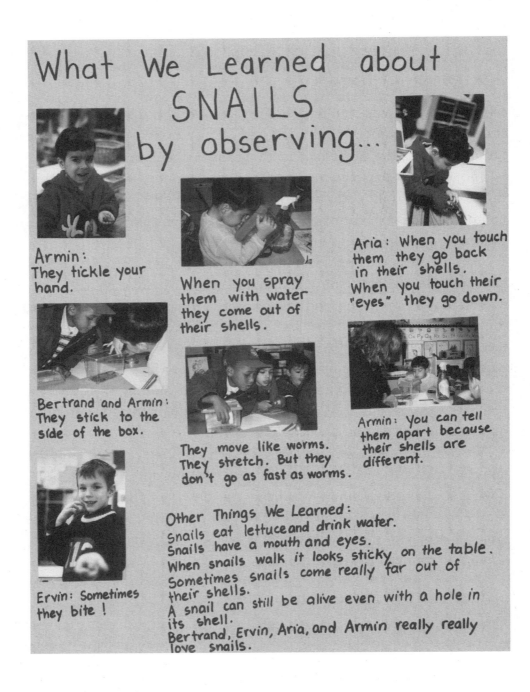

What We Learned about SNAILS by observing...

Armin: They tickle your hand.

When you spray them with water they come out of their shells.

Aria: When you touch them they go back in their shells. When you touch their "eyes" they go down.

Bertrand and Armin: They stick to the side of the box.

They move like worms. They stretch. But they don't go as fast as worms.

Armin: You can tell them apart because their shells are different.

Ervin: Sometimes they bite!

Other Things We Learned:
Snails eat lettuce and drink water.
Snails have a mouth and eyes.
When snails walk it looks sticky on the table.
Sometimes snails come really far out of their shells.
A snail can still be alive even with a hole in its shell.
Bertrand, Ervin, Aria, and Armin really really love snails.

A Word About Design Technology

Although this book is about science teaching and learning, many aspects of technology teaching and learning are closely connected to what children do when they do science.

The *National Science Education Standards* distinguishes science and technology as follows: "The central distinguishing characteristic between science and technology is a difference in goal: the goal of science is to understand the natural world, and the goal of technology is to make modifications in the world to meet human needs" (National Research Council 1996, 24). The process of design technology is much like that of science inquiry. Young children might well be called "natural designers." Their work often includes questions such as "How does this work?" "How can I make this go farther?" "How can I build this higher?" Their play is full of inventions, designs, and construction.

Distinguishing between science and technology, or labeling children's work as "technology," is unnecessary and inappropriate at this age. But teachers can encourage young children to think about their work from the perspective of design technology as well as from the perspective of science inquiry. They can support children's ideas whether the children want to make a container for their rock collection, a telescope to look at the sky, or a portable home for a living critter. By providing materials and serving as a sounding board and guide, teachers can encourage young children to follow through on their ideas while challenging them to think about how things work, what materials work best, problems that arise, and alternate solutions they might explore.

CHAPTER 3

Life Science in the Early Childhood Classroom

Young children are fascinated by the living things they encounter around them. Life science for young children is about maintaining this fascination through the close and often systematic observation of plants and animals, including themselves. It is about guiding children to begin to think about living things—what they look like, how they live, and how they change. That is, the life science program in the early childhood classroom focuses both on the characteristics of an organism and how it lives in its natural environment outside of the classroom. At the same time, it encourages children to treat all things and their environments with care and respect.

Doing Inquiry

Children's study of the living world around them is very much like the work of naturalists. Naturalists identify and describe the plants and animals they find. They observe and record the lives of different organisms and their relationships with one another and with the surrounding environment. This kind of inquiry has a strong basis in observation and recording. As children engage in life science, they use their senses, magnifiers, measuring tools, and notepads. They measure, count, make observational drawings, and even begin to map what they have seen where. As children share their observations and think about what they have seen, they start to sort and categorize, classify, look for patterns, and raise questions about the living things they have come to know.

Children's study of living things takes time. Watching a plant grow and change takes days and weeks, not minutes or hours. Observing and reflecting on the life cycle of an organism may take even longer, and seeing the changes that happen from season to season can be a yearlong study. Given young children's focus on the present, it is a challenge to make some of these changes truly visible to them. But their own documentation and recording, along with teachers' documentation and ongoing classroom discussion, can provide a bridge from week to week and even from month to month.

Engaging with Content

A life science program provides children with ongoing opportunities to observe living things in their environment and begin to appreciate the diversity and variation of organisms that exist. It allows children to develop their ideas about the characteristics of living things including their basic needs, life cycles, and their dependence on one another and on the environment.

From their experiences with pets and animals inside and outside the home, children develop ideas about living things. Research on children's thinking provides some clues to some of the most common theories children develop. For example, many young children often focus on one simple criterion—movement—to make the distinction between what is alive and what is not alive. Windup cars are alive because they move "on their own." Similarly, plants may not be considered alive. Young children may also be working on ideas about whether people are animals; many do not think so. But at the same time, they will often interpret the needs and behaviors of animals in very human terms.

Teachers' close observation of children will reveal other interesting theories children have constructed. With an understanding of children's thinking about living things and clear goals in mind, teachers can create experiences and guide children to a deeper awareness and understanding of the living world around them. By encouraging children to observe more closely and notice patterns in what they see, children can begin to refine their ideas, laying the foundation for more reasoned and evidence-based theories of life.

In the following pages, we describe major content areas of life science for young children. We suggest the kinds of experiences children can engage in, the ideas they can explore, and brief descriptions of some of the more common theories children hold. The content areas are separated to help teachers set goals and guide children's experiences, but in most cases, these areas will be integrated in classroom work.

Physical Characteristics of Living Things

The physical characteristics of plants and animals include details of color, shape, and texture, as well as their different parts. As children observe plants and animals closely, they can begin to think and talk about how the parts of plants and animals are useful to them in meeting their needs and how the parts often reflect what the animal does. For example, the shape of the worm helps it tunnel through the earth; the long legs of the rabbit help it jump, and the squirrel's long tail helps it balance as it runs through the tree branches. The roots of the plant hold it up and take in water; the antennae of the snail help it find its way.

Young children's attention is often focused on one or maybe two salient features of an organism. For example, one child's drawing of a leaf may focus on its shape. Another child's drawing may focus more on the leaf's bright yellow color than on its shape. Teachers can help children observe living things' physical characteristics more closely by asking children to describe an organism in greater detail or compare how two or more organisms look alike and different, as well as by encouraging representational drawing.

The Basic Needs of Living Things

All living things have basic needs that must be met for them to grow, develop, and survive. Most animals need food, water, air, and a safe place to live. Most plants need light and water and air, too, but they don't eat food as animals do; rather, they make it. How organisms meet their needs varies enormously. By studying and comparing the needs of a few kinds of plants and animals, children can begin to realize that some needs are basic to all animals or to all plants. They can also see that there are similarities and differences in how living things meet their needs. Some kinds of plants need more water or less light than others. Different kinds of animals need different kinds of food and shelter. Children may also discover that if plants' and animals' needs are not met, they will die.

Many children may realize that animals have needs and require care, but with little experience actually caring for animals and given the focus at this age on self, they are likely to think that animals' needs are similar to their own. For example, children might say that the snail needs a bed, the rabbit needs a place to play, or the guinea pig needs its mommy and daddy. Asking children to think about the difference between wants and needs is one way to challenge these ideas; holding discussions outdoors where children can observe animals in their natural habitats or building a terrarium indoors are others.

Homes and classrooms often have plants on window sills, and watering them may be a familiar activity to many young children. But if questioned about the needs of plants, young children may suggest that plants also need food and assume that they get it from the soil. Growing plants in water can raise interesting questions about how plants actually get food.

Simple Behaviors

Animals meet their needs by living in a particular place and by behaving in particular ways. Movement is very important and relates to the places the animals live and how their bodies are shaped. As children observe organisms closely in the environment and in the classroom, they can see behaviors such as how worms move through the earth to get their food, how pill bugs curl up when they are threatened, and how spiders spin webs to catch their food. Plants don't move around and behave like animals, but they do react to their environments. Children can do simple experiments to see that plants will bend toward the light or grow tall and skinny if the soil isn't rich enough.

Young children have likely heard many stories in which animals behave as people do. Children are also still quite egocentric. As a result, they are likely to attribute intentionality to animal behavior that is like their own. For example, children may talk about spiders playing in their webs or about worms that kiss. Teachers can help children follow up on these ideas through discussion and close observation. For example, by asking children to observe what spiders do in the webs, teachers can encourage children to reflect on their observations and refine their thinking.

Life Cycles

All living things change over time. Some changes are very slow and happen over years, like the growth of a tree or a large animal. Other changes happen more quickly, over the course of a few weeks, such as the germination of a seedling or the metamorphosis of a caterpillar or tadpole. Still others seem immediate, like losing a tooth. Many changes are related to the life cycle. Plants and animals are born, they grow and develop, they reproduce, and they die. Children can observe some of these stages of the life cycle and, in some cases, see the changes and transformations that occur. Observing these changes can help to expand their ideas about what is alive.

Young children have ideas about some of the stages of the life cycle, including growth and development, based on their own experience of growth from baby to toddler to young child or their experiences with younger siblings or pets. But given children's focus on specific events in the present and their immature sense of time, they are unlikely to have a sense of the cycle of life stages or the universality of the life cycle. Moreover, they are likely to view stages of the life cycle, such as birth and death, as magical or unpredictable. Providing children with the opportunity to see the life cycle in several organisms in the classroom can enrich children's experience and extend their thinking. For example, children can plant beans, tend them, watch them grow and develop, and harvest the beans to plant again. They can observe stages of the life cycle by watching monarch or painted lady butterflies change from larva to butterfly in a few weeks, or observe snails reproduce in the classroom terrarium.

Variation and Diversity

There are many kinds of living things. Even in a small area, there are various species of bugs; there are small mammals; there are trees, bushes, and smaller plants. Young children can begin to group living things based on their similarities and differences. Teachers can guide children to group living things into very large categories, such as plants and animals. Other categories can be more specific, such as trees, bushes, and small plants; animals that live in the ground, on the ground, and above the ground. Other categories might be plants that have leaves and plants that don't; animals that have many legs and animals that have two or four or six; animals with fur and without fur.

Categorizing encourages children to focus on the many physical characteristics of organisms, and it provides a foundation for future understanding of the scientific classification of organisms.

Children's organizational structures and categories are still limited at this age; their criteria are usually based on their experiences and some of the visual characteristics of the living things around them. They are likely to invent their own categories based on unscientific criteria, such as what they like or don't like or plants that are tall and plants that are short. Their plant category may not include trees; the animal category will probably not include people. Although these categories may not be scientific, the children are developing their skills in categorization, and it is important for teachers to accept and discuss the process with them by posing questions such as, "What is special about this group? How is this group different from that? Where does this animal go and why?"

As children focus more closely on living things by describing and representing them, they begin to recognize subtler differences and appreciate the diversity around them. A closer look at organisms of the same species can highlight the variation that exists. If children compare the leaves on one tree, they can see that the leaves may have the same shape but vary in size depending on where they are on the tree. The spots on one ladybug may be different from those on another. If children focus on themselves and their classmates, they can see that each child in the class looks different, but all have many similarities.

Relationship Between Living Things and Their Environments

Through the observation of living things, children can begin to think about how living things depend on other living and nonliving things for some of their needs. For example, squirrels need trees to live in and nuts to eat; plants grow better when worms make tunnels and holes in the soil; foxes eat rabbits; and many animals eat specific plants. Living things also depend on certain conditions in the environment, such as water for drinking and safe places for hiding. As young children think more deeply about living things and their needs, they may begin to understand that if people disturb the environment too much, some living things may not be able to meet their needs and will move or die out.

People

While it may take time to realize that people are animals, children can focus their attention on many of the similarities between themselves and animals during their close observations of living things. Through their discussions and investigations, they can begin to understand some complex ideas—that all people are basically similar, but each person is also unique; that the human body is made up of different parts and each is important for doing certain things; that the senses are very important for taking in information about the world. Teachers can help children focus on people's observable characteristics: how they are the same and how they vary from person to person. By encouraging children to compare these characteristics to those of other animals, children can begin to notice similarities and differences. At the same time, children can begin to realize how people and other animals share the same need for food, water, air, and shelter, and they can consider how these needs can be met in many ways.

Children also are likely to be interested in what is inside their bodies—internal organs, blood, and bones—and how their bodies work. This makes for interesting discussion, but because of the complexity of body systems and the fact that they cannot be seen, it is difficult for children to explore these ideas in depth.

The stories that follow vividly illustrate how two teachers from very different classrooms engaged their children in yearlong explorations of living things. Ms. Howard and Miss Scott each chose a different focus of study—one chose animals, the other plants—but they shared a common goal: to help children explore important life science ideas. Both teachers provide children with many opportunities to observe organisms closely and develop their understandings about their basic needs, life cycles, dependence on one another and on the environment, and the diversity and variation of organisms that exist.

The stories illustrate how teachers can take on the tasks of creating a classroom environment and culture that conveys the excitement and wonder of observing and learning about living things. At the same time, they demonstrate many strategies teachers can use to focus and deepen children's experiences and thinking. They also show how children can develop specific skills, such as how to use magnifiers, make observational drawings, use scientific vocabulary, and record data.

In the Classroom with Ms. Howard

Ms. Howard teaches four- and five-year-old children in an urban public school. She has a group of twenty children who come from many different racial and ethnic groups; 70 percent are from families of low socioeconomic status. The building is an old brick school from the 1930s with a hardtop playground surrounded by a small strip of land with a few trees and weeds growing against the chain-link fence that surrounds the area.

In the past, Ms. Howard always had classroom pets, but she was concerned that the children's interactions with the pets were focused on making homes for the animals, cuddling them, and drawing pictures of their friend, the hamster. Although she engaged them in thinking about what the pets needed, the conditions in the classroom were far from the real conditions in which these creatures might have lived in the wild. Ms. Howard also was concerned that the "homes" in the classroom felt more like cages to the animals.

Ms. Howard was determined to take a different direction this year, focusing more on what the children could find outdoors, the diversity of the animals, and the relationship of each living thing to its particular environment. The study of living things will last through October, taper off during the winter, and then begin again in the spring when living things begin to reappear.

Beginning Outdoors

In this first segment of this four-part story, Ms. Howard describes the events and her thoughts as she started the year with a study of animals outdoors in their natural environment.

I needed to get the kids ready for this focus on living things and their environment. To get myself ready, I spent a lot of time in the schoolyard, really looking at what plants and animals were there. I also talked with the children about what it means to be a naturalist, and how being a naturalist is different than going out to run and play. I explained that naturalists are a special kind of scientist who go outdoors to look for different plants and animals, but are careful not to disturb them in their homes.

We also talked about how naturalists use tools to find living things and look at them really, really closely. Before I took the children out for their naturalist expeditions, I wanted to make sure they had opportunities to interact with the tools. I gave them hand lenses and we talked about what they're used for. I gave them magazines so they could practice using the hand lenses to look at pictures that don't move. And I tried to instill the idea that we'd be looking for living things, so we needed to be careful not to hurt what we found. But saying "be careful" might not mean a lot to a three-year-old or a four-year-old. So before we went outside we did a lot of work with Popsicle® sticks, another of our tools, having them practice safe ways of picking up rubber bugs without cutting them in half!

Once all the children had experience using the tools and we had talked about some of the "rules," we were ready to go out. I gathered them together and said, "Now we're going to be naturalists! We're going to go outside to look carefully at plants and animals. And we're going to bring our tools with us, the hand lenses and the Popsicle® sticks. What plants and animals do you think we'll find?" The kids predicted they'd find butterflies and snakes and flowers and even vampires. No one thought we would find worms. But that's exactly what Jorge and Peter found.

We went outside a couple of times a week for several weeks. Before every outdoor expedition, I'd ask the same questions to get them to think about what different organisms they had seen and where they had found them. "What did we find last time? Where did we find it? What did we find out about them?" and "What living things do you think we'll find today?" The children really got into looking for worms. Whenever someone found a worm, we all knew. The "worm finders" would shriek or holler and everyone would gather around to see. I asked the young naturalists to show me how they could use their tools to look at the worms carefully.

I responded to the children's worm findings by saying, "Where did you find this? What is the worm's home like? How did you find it?" And I tried to make connections among the children's findings. Initially, the children dug in random places. Eventually, they began to figure out patterns and become more intentional in their worm searches. They'd say, "Oh, this is a good digging hole," or "I found worms under leaves before, so let's look here."

Some children did find other small creatures as well—ants, a beetle, some small grubs. Sometimes the kids wanted to bring indoors the living things they found—their "jewels." The last thing they wanted to do was to leave it so somebody else would find it the next day. Malea didn't just find a worm—it was *her* worm. The next time we went out after that, Peter found a worm and Malea immediately said, "Hey, that's *my* worm. You found *my* worm." I asked, "How do you know that's your worm?" She said, " 'Cause it's pink and long." I said, "Let's use our tools and look really closely. Show me. What do you see that lets you know that this is the same worm you found yesterday?" Over time, as the children saw many worms, they began to realize that all the worms had similar qualities. They no longer did the "my worm" thing. They recognized that worms have many characteristics in common and there was no way of knowing if it was the exact worm that they had found the day before.

One child in my class, Sonia, came to this exploration with lots of experience studying living things. She had "entomologist" written all over her, and the whole class soon recognized that, too. She just knew how to handle bugs and she wasn't the least bit intimidated. And when kids found an insect, they looked for Sonia. "What's this?" they'd ask her. "What do you know about it? Where can we find more?" Listening to the children and what they were asking helped me to better understand and follow up on their questions. For example, I asked Ann why she thought her little slug was under the pile of leaves and where she thought she might look for others.

Figure 3–1 *Ms. Howard asked: "Where did you find this? What is the worm's home like?"*

During the early part of our study, my student intern noticed a dead mouse on the edge of the playground. Panic-stricken, she said, "We have to get this mouse out of here before the kids see it!" But I said, "No," that this was an opportunity for the kids to think about living and dead. And anyway, when would be the next time they would have a chance to see a beheaded dead mouse? So the children who were interested gathered around the mouse. Some said, "Eweeee," but they were fascinated too. And we talked. When Keisha said the mouse was dead, I asked, "How do you know?" She responded, "It's not moving," which I realized was the major factor children used to judge whether something was alive or not. Others said, "Pieces are gone," or "There's blood." And then there was a lot of speculation about what happened to the mouse and how it had died.

Over time, the process of inquiry and reflection became a part of our classroom culture, part of our routine. For instance, after each outdoor exploration, we made lists of what the children had found. I'd say, "Terry, you said you found a worm. I'm going to write that down and make a naturalist's drawing of the worm you found. I want the drawing to look like the worm. Tell me what marker I should use, and how I should draw it." I'd draw a picture, always checking in to see if the picture reflected what they saw. The children never held back from saying, "No, it was skinnier," or "The head was pointy," or "You need lines." Sometimes the children drew the animal, too. And sometimes the kids had debates about an animal's color or its shapes, and their debates led to new questions that we would follow up on the next time we went out.

Over time, I asked new questions that went beyond description: "What do you think the animal is doing? Why do you think he moved like that?"

After weeks of having firsthand experiences finding and observing living things (and some dead ones too), the children's observations became more detailed and their predictions changed. No one predicted that they'd see vampires or snakes anymore. They now based their predictions on what they had seen before, and their predictions became more specific, more detailed—more scientific. They moved from guessing they'd see snakes and vampires to expecting to find "black ants," "skinny worms," or a "dead mouse."

Ms. Howard had a clear sense of purpose—for the children to find and closely observe the small animals in the yard—that guided what she did in the beginning weeks. She also encouraged them to think

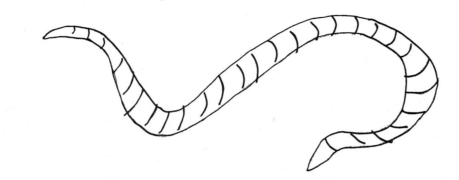

Terry found a worm on the playground under the leaves. The head was pointy and the worm had lines.

Figure 3-2 *Ms. Howard's Recording of a Child's Observation*

about two basic life science concepts: (1) diversity and variation and (2) the relationship of each living thing to its particular environment. By doing so, she actively created an environment of respect for living things and an atmosphere in which the children were encouraged to observe closely, using their senses and simple tools.

The children's interest in finding more worms became the context for encouraging a small group to think about the places the worms were found and where the children might find others. Ms. Howard did not give in to the children's desire to have pet worms for a number of reasons: She wanted the children to first explore and observe the animals in their natural environments and to begin to understand and respect the animals' needs before bringing them in for a short time to observe them more closely.

Observation is a critical part of scientific inquiry. But Ms. Howard realized that adult guidance is essential in helping children develop their observational skills. When the children began talking about "their worms," Ms. Howard used the opportunity to encourage them to look more closely at the variation in worms. As they focused on what they were actually seeing, the children came to realize that while there were some differences, for the most part, worms were very similar. In fact, it was often difficult, and sometimes impossible, to distinguish one worm from another. Ms. Howard also helped the children to go beyond their initial observations of one or two salient characteristics by continually probing for specific details as the children shared their observations and as she and the children talked about their drawings.

Developing the children's ability to use tools also became an inquiry focus. Within the dramatic context of becoming a naturalist, Ms. Howard taught the children to use several tools properly. Although Ms. Howard did not frequently use a direct teaching approach, she knew that careful preparation would allow the children to observe more closely, respect the tools, and, above all, begin to respect the creatures they were about to study. Naturalists use drawing and sketching as well as field notes as critical tools for gathering data in the field. By drawing with the children, Ms. Howard was modeling the process of observational drawing with its focus on detail and accuracy.

At the start of this exploration, Ms. Howard struck a balance between nurturing the children's interests as they explored the outdoor environment and directly teaching skills that the children could apply to their explorations. While supporting the children's excitement in what they found, she also carefully set the stage with clear instruction about tools and careful handling of any small animals. She gently guided the children toward more focused observations and thought about where they found their animals.

In a real inquiry into living things in the environment, much is unpredictable. Ms. Howard was quick to take advantage of the unplanned event of the dead mouse. She saw the dead mouse as an opportunity to raise a critical question for children of this age: What is dead and what is not dead?

Moving Indoors

During the next phase of the exploration, Ms. Howard decided to move the naturalist work indoors by building a classroom terrarium for worms. The timing seemed right. The children had already had lots of opportunities to observe animals in the natural environment—observing where they live and how they meet their basic needs.

By bringing the worms indoors, the children could learn more about worms' physical characteristics and behaviors through closer observation.

Once it started getting cold and it was harder to find animals, we needed to bring some indoors for more careful investigation. Worms were the natural choice because so many of the children had seen them and found them outdoors; they are relatively easy to keep indoors; they don't jump or fly; and they're big enough for the kids to really see them. But I didn't want to just dig up the worms and bring them in. I wanted to use this as an opportunity to help the kids really think about how they could study plants and animals indoors. I said, "You've been naturalists outdoors. Now that it's getting colder, let's think about how you can study your worms indoors, as indoor naturalists!" I also explained that naturalists always make sure that living things have a good place to live inside—a place that feels like their outdoor home. Then I asked, "What should we do to make the worms feel at home in our classroom?" One child yelled out, "Grass. They need grass." "How do you know?" I asked. She answered, "That's where I found my worm." "I also remember that you had to dig to find worms. How come you had to dig?" Another child

What We Think We Need
for Our Terrarium

dirt

dirt is ground

rocks

sticks

worms

leaves

Figure 3–3 *What We Think We Need for Our Terrarium*

said, "That's where they live." I pushed a little further. "Where do they live?" Several children called out, "In the ground. In the dirt." "Oh," I said, "So we need dirt to make the worms feel at home!"

Then I remembered the *Salamander Room*, a book by Anne Mazer about a boy who imagines how he can keep a salamander in his house by transforming his room into a jungle. I read the book to the children and it was perfect, because it focused on the importance of creating an indoor environment that meets an animal's needs. At the same time, there was an element of fantasy that may have made some children think, "OK, if we bring in these worms, we can turn our classroom into a forest!" After I read the book, I told them we weren't going to turn our whole classroom into a home for worms, but we needed to be sure we had thought about everything the worms would need. I asked, "How many rocks should we collect? And how big should they be? And what about the sticks? How many sticks should we get?"

After lots of discussions and research, we headed outdoors with our list in hand. Pairs of kids were assigned to collect different things. The "dirt collectors" picked out "really good dirt." (A few times I asked them what they meant by "good dirt" but they were too intent on digging and collecting to engage in any conversation at that point.) The "stick collectors" and the "rock collectors" carefully picked small sticks that the worms could climb on. The children really worked together, though ones with strong personalities, usually the older ones, would often take the lead and become the directors. Those were the children who were saying, "That stick is too big," or "Somebody go find a good rock."

I was a bit overwhelmed with organizing the making of the terrarium. I decided to make two and work with groups of four children at a time. So when the kids were done collecting, I put an empty terrarium on the floor and the groups decided where everything went—they were designers now. Each group got to do something and each child got to put in one thing that he or she had collected from the outdoors. The kids then dug up seventeen worms and put them in the terraria that they had so carefully constructed.

The children's ongoing explorations of the outdoors had provided them with a sense of familiarity with the living things in their environment. Ms. Howard's questions, discussions, and drawings, as well as the children's discussions among themselves, kept the focus on important ideas of variation and diversity in what they were finding and the idea that organisms live in particular places. Making a home for a few visitors to the classroom provided the context and motivation to build on these ideas and to use the children's experiences to focus in on the needs of living things and, in particular, the needs of worms. It also was an opportunity to challenge the children to think about what they had experienced, and draw from their experience to solve a problem.

Direct hands-on experience is important, but it is by discussing and reflecting on that experience that new understanding emerges. Discussions with young children are certainly easiest in small groups while they are working, or immediately afterward. Large-group discussions can also be valuable, providing children with opportunities to share their thinking and hear the perspectives of others.

Managing such large-group discussions can be a challenge, but teachers can use a number of strategies to engage young children in meaningful ways, for instance, reading an appropriate book. *The Salamander Room*, a book with elements of fantasy, offered the children in Ms. Howard's class an opportunity to focus on what animals need, while inviting their imaginations to soar. Ms. Howard also could have chosen a book about how to care for animals indoors.

Figure 3–4 *Two Rock Collectors*

Discussions provided Ms. Howard with an opportunity to assess her group's understandings of guiding concepts, in this case, the basic needs of living things, the importance of the environment in meeting those needs, and some of the behaviors of worms in meeting those needs. Along with records of children's conversations and questions, group discussions helped her identify concepts the children were struggling with and plan ways to follow up.

The Study of Worm Behavior

With the terraria completed, Ms. Howard was ready to help the children focus on the worms and their behaviors, while helping them to notice patterns of behavior and changes in the organisms.

After the terraria were complete with worms, I wanted the children to really think about how worms act and why. To get the children thinking about worm behavior, I asked the kids to draw their predictions about how they thought the terraria would look in the morning. Would anything be different? What would the worms be doing in there? The kids drew their pictures of worms on sticks and rocks. They said, "The worms will be on my stick," or "They'll be on my rock." It was like they thought, "Why wouldn't the worms want to be on my stick? After all, I picked out this stick just for them."

The first thing that the children did when they came in the next day was look in the terraria, but no worms were to be seen. Some of the younger kids pronounced, "Someone stole all our worms!" Others said, "Let's check under the rock one more time." Some children were detectives, making speculations, then finding the holes in the speculations they made. When one child said, "They must've crawled out," another child asked, "But how could they get out? 'Cause we had really fat worms and these are little skinny holes on the top of this thing." Sonia suddenly said, "You need to look underground." So the kids got their tools and starting digging. This was almost a disaster as the kids had created this great environment. I had to quickly say no trowels, only Popsicle® sticks, and only two searchers at each terrarium at a time or we would have had dirt and worms everywhere.

Oh, the relief on their faces when they found all seventeen worms! Some of the kids started making connections that they hadn't before, saying, "Yeah, that's where we found them outside." But the conversation didn't end there. I asked, "Why do you think the worms go underground?" Some children said, "'Cause they like it.' Cause they live there." Others said that if worms were on the ground, people could step on them because they're not fast enough to get away.

I probed some more, asking, "But how did the worms get underground? You say they crawled underground? But the dirt is pretty hard. How is it that something with no arms and legs could get under the dirt like that?" All the kids were really into figuring out how the worms could get underground. Then I asked, "What do you think would happen if we put the worms on the dirt right now? What do you think the worms would do?" Doing an experiment was the kids' idea. They said we could put dirt on trays, then put worms on the dirt to see what they would do. So that's what they did. The kids watched the worms really closely. "It's moving with its tummy." They noticed how their bodies got skinny and pointy as they pushed themselves under the dirt. Their observations led to other questions. "Why does a worm get shorter when you touch it? Why do they wiggle? Why do they move like crazy sometimes, just thrashing around? How do they move?"

We kept talking about what the kids knew about worms and about what they wanted to know (see Figure 3–5 on page 42). Their questions were interesting, and there was quite a range. One child, maybe just to be silly, asked, "How do worms kiss?" What my student intern did was interesting. She followed up by saying, "Let's look closely. What did you see? Do they kiss?" I thought that was great because in some way she was saying, "Let's not assume that they kiss. Let's find out if they do kiss."

But the children didn't just ask questions; we also pursued those questions. The whole-class focus was how worms moved, but I always kept the kids' questions in mind as they observed worms, and their questions guided my interactions with them. For example, when I was with Rae-Anna, I'd say, "I remember you wanted to know how worms eat. Let's watch and see what this worm does. So how do you think we can figure out how the worms eat?" I also related the children's questions to what we had found in books, and I was constantly trying to connect the children's observations by saying things like, "Rae-Anna wants to know how worms eat. Sonia, maybe you can help us. You said you saw a worm's mouth this morning. Can you tell us what you saw?"

Throughout the exploration, I encouraged the children to record what they had noticed by making observational drawings. And the kids drew for a purpose, to record the evidence, to capture the details of what they had seen. One thing I love about worms is that everybody can draw a worm, which means that kids don't get caught up in "I can't draw."

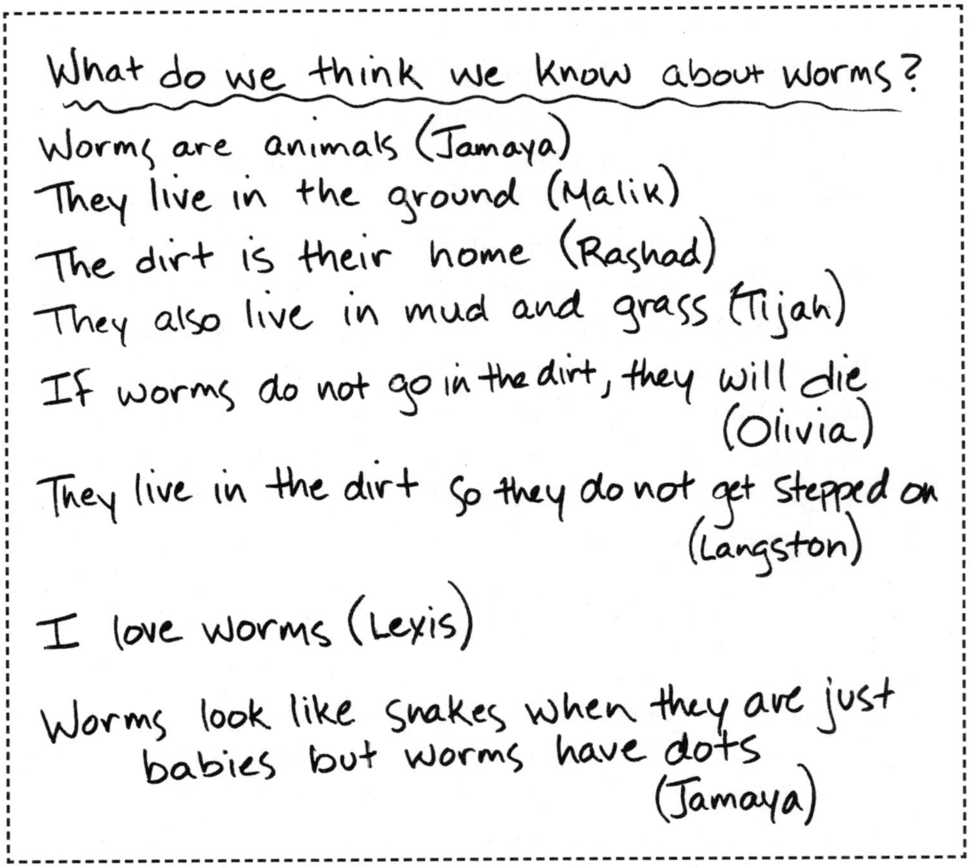

What do we think we know about worms?

Worms are animals (Jamaya)

They live in the ground (Malik)

The dirt is their home (Rashad)

They also live in mud and grass (Tijah)

If worms do not go in the dirt, they will die
(Olivia)

They live in the dirt so they do not get stepped on
(Langston)

I love worms (Lexis)

Worms look like snakes when they are just
babies but worms have dots
(Jamaya)

Figure 3–5 *What do we think know about worms?*

And because worms have such a simple body structure, I could really see the range in what the kids could do. Some would just draw a brown line. And then there's Eddie. He's one of the older children in my class, and he views himself as an artist. He can look at something and represent it pretty clearly. So Eddie would be looking at this really simple creature that has no legs—essentially just a tube—and he would capture all the details, including the lines on the worm, the little ridge near the worm's head. And he'd even draw the worm crawling out of the ground!

The children drew in their journals. I then talked to them about their drawings, and they dictated what they wanted me to write. They dictated things like: "Worms wrap around each other. Worms crawl in the soil. They are squiggly and slinky. Worms don't run because they don't have feet. They grow like people: bigger, longer, and fatter. Some worms are babies and some are not. They live in the dirt because the sun will dry them out. Worms eat with their mouths." We date-stamped the journals

What do I want to know about worms?

How do worms hug? (Jamaya)
Do worms kiss on the mouth? (Tijah)
Do worms crawl? (Fiona)
Do worms have feet? (Malia)
How do worms eat? (Rae-Anna)
How do worms run? (Klancy)
Do worms run?
How do worms grow? (Jamaya)
How do worms play? (Kashe)
Are worms babies? (Olivia)
How do worms fight? (Jan)
Why do worms live in the dirt? (Ms. Bono)
Do mother worms feed their babies? (Malik)
How do worms cross the street? (Nacaira)

Figure 3–6 *What do I want to know about worms?*

every time the kids wrote or drew in them, so we could keep track of how the children's observations changed over time (see Figure 3–7 on page 44).

And we talked a lot, not just when we were watching the worms, but during circle time, too. I'm big on having the kids describe things. I always push for more details, saying, "Tell us with your words," or "Point with your words." At first, the kids got exasperated, but then some just got in the habit of providing details, using words and their bodies, too. I remember when we were talking about how worms move, how they stretch out and get small. The kids were using their whole bodies to show what the worm looks like when it moves, which isn't easy because people can't stretch the way worms do. One of the kids tried to compare how a worm moves to a toy he had seen. English is his second language, so he used his hands to show how the toy moved, in and out, in and out.

Matthew

OCT 15 2000

Worms like to eat rotten corn and apples.

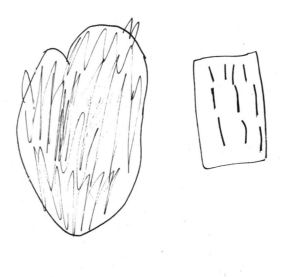

Figure 3–7 *Four-Year-Old Child's Journal Page*

That's when another kid said, "Oh, you mean a Slinky®!" I was blown away. I mean, I never would have thought of that, but it was a perfect analogy.

After school, I headed for the toy store and bought a Slinky®. The next day, we played with the Slinky® and talked about its movement, and that expanded everyone's thinking about worms. That is, the worm just doesn't get skinny and kind of sharp when it goes under the dirt. The worm's body also pushes, by stretching out, pulling in, and then pushing down with its head.

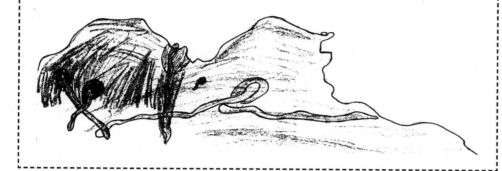

Eddie   OCT 17 2000

**Worms use their heads to
go in the dirt.**

Figure 3–8 *Six-Year-Old Child's Journal Page*

If teachers do not keep children focused on learning about worms, even *worms* can become classroom pets that children play with and nurture rather than something they observe and study. Ms. Howard had thought about behavior, and movement in particular, as a focus for exploration because many children had been intrigued by the way the animals moved (see Figure 3–9 on page 46). But she waited for the right moment and then watched it catch on. This discussion of the "found" worms provided the opportunity, and the children responded. But the children had many other questions and interests as well. As she said, not all the questions could be explored, but there were several that could be, such as, "How do worms eat?" or "Do worms run?" Other questions could be looked up in a book, such as, "Do mother worms feed their babies?" And still others could be thought about and discussed in groups, such as, "Why do worms live in the dirt?"

Little of inquiry in life science for children at this age is experimental, but Ms. Howard was quick to take advantage of the opportunity to do the "experiment" the children suggested to see what would happen if the worms were placed on the dirt. Moments such as these

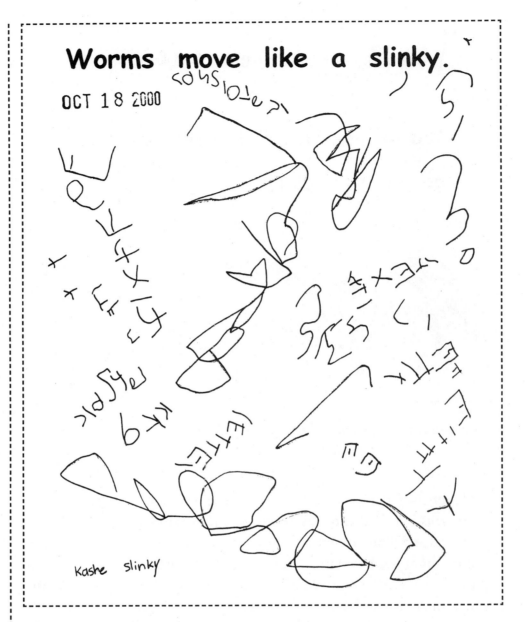

Figure 3–9 *Four-Year-Old Child's Journal Page*

are important ones in helping children to see themselves as real science learners, able to follow up on their own questions.

Collecting information or data and continually reflecting on that data is important in deepening children's thinking about living things and developing their skills as observers. Ms. Howard encouraged the children to use observational drawing as a naturalist tool, adding characteristics they saw and not including those they did not see. Imaginative drawings of worms with smiles and multicolored bodies have their place in the art corner but not in the science notebook.

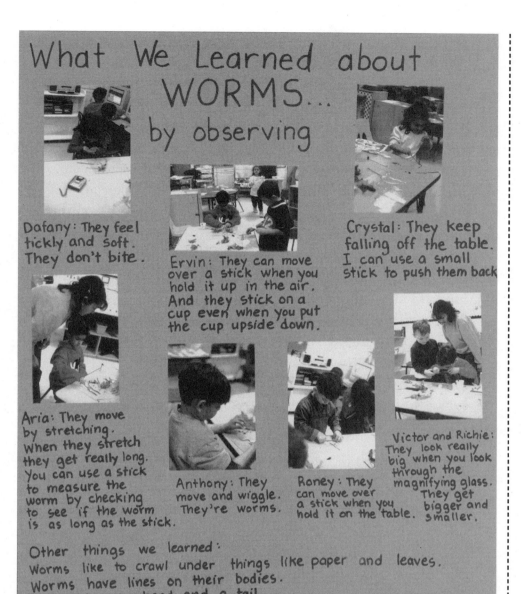

Figure 3–10 *Capturing Children's Learning About Worms*

Focus on the Life Cycle

By November the children's interest in worms started to wane. After a discussion with the children about the needs of their worms and a quick call to the local nature center for advice, it was agreed that Ms. Howard would take the worms home and dig them into her compost pile. During the winter months, Ms. Howard turned to other science explorations. But in early spring, she began to plan her study of animals again.

It can be very exciting for children to see the life cycle of an animal, but it is not easy. Small mammals, such as guinea pigs and mice, may reproduce in the classroom, but it is difficult to create an appropriate environment. Other animals such as snails or worms will reproduce and children can watch this growth and development occur. Ms. Howard chose another kind of life cycle, one in which animals go through specific stages—metamorphosis. This can be very exciting and dramatize the growth process. Some teachers keep mealworms so children can see the change from worm to beetle. Others have been successful with frog eggs, watching them become tadpoles and then frogs. Ms. Howard chose monarch butterflies.

In the episode below, she describes how, over four weeks, the children watched the caterpillars (larvae) that had hatched from eggs grow larger, change (pupate) into a chrysalis (pupa of a butterfly), and then emerge from the chrysalis as a butterfly. This was not the full life cycle—only from larva to butterfly—but it was a fascinating experience.

I ordered a monarch butterfly kit from a catalog, and when it arrived I gathered the children around it in a circle. I showed them the little box with larvae inside. I told them that there were butterflies in the box, but before we opened it, we should make a chart listing what they know about butterflies. Some children said butterflies were once caterpillars. Others talked about how they became cocoons before they became butterflies.

Then I asked the children to think about what the butterflies would look like when we opened the box. They said the butterflies would have wings. Beautiful, beautiful wings. So when we opened the box, the children said, "Hey, those aren't butterflies!" I told them they didn't look like butterflies, but they were butterflies—just at a different stage. And I tried to relate it to their own lives, saying that they don't look the same now as when they were babies and they would look different when they grew up. These were baby butterflies that had hatched four or five days ago from eggs. I told them we could call them caterpillars or larvae. Ben said they looked like our worms. Later he and three others had to go outside, find worms, and bring them back in to compare.

I wanted the children to think about the needs of the caterpillars and also to think back to our work with worms. So during our science talk I said that the larvae would be OK in the box for a few days, but we needed to make them feel at home. I showed them our documentation panel from our worm study, saying, "We figured out what our worms needed, so we made them a home like the one we found them in. But the caterpillars came to us in a box! How are we going to find out what kind of outside home they like, so we can build one in here?"

Then I showed the children the book that came with the kit and a library book I found in the reference section about providing for butterflies indoors. Together, the children and I looked through the books. We figured out that we would need a supply of fresh milkweed to feed the larvae, a large container so the adult butterflies would be able to spread their wings and move about, and sugar water for the butterflies to drink. I also told the children about how, the year before, a naturalist had shown me how to make a tent so that we could really see what was happening with the larvae and so the butterflies would have space to fly. The next day, we built two tentlike structures out of gauze and cardboard so the children could watch the larvae grow and change.

The children were fascinated with the larvae. During the day, while other things were going on, a few children at a time would gather by the structures and look for a moment or two. My aide and I would try to stop by as well, to show our interest and model close observation. I think just about every child would take a look at least once every couple of days. And at least twice a week, I would take time during circle time at the end of the day to talk about what the children had seen, what had changed ("They're getting bigger and bigger"), and what the kids thought they would do next.

I started a big book and invited the children to draw the larvae. Each drawing was dated and put into the big book. I was amazed at what they did. Sometimes one child would start drawing, and that enticed another to do the same thing. And some children were drawing and talking about the caterpillar.

Three of the older children who had just turned five decided to make their own books about their own larvae. They each picked one larva and measured it every couple of days. I helped them make little cutouts the size of each larva. It was great way for them and the others to actually see how much the larvae had grown.

About a week later Marie came running over to say that a spider must have come into our classroom in the middle of the night and made a web in the caterpillar's tent. We all gathered around and talked about what was there. I said, "Let's look really, really closely and see if we can get any clues about where it came from." We could actually see the lar-

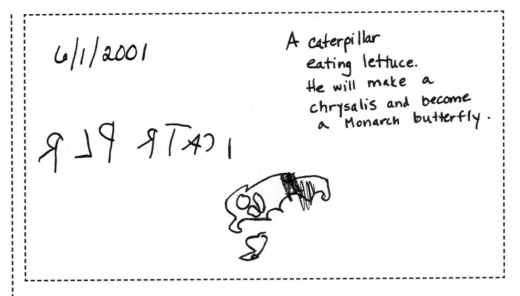

Figure 3-11 *A Page in the Big Book by Ella, Age Four*

vae spinning stuff. "Hey," Marie said. "That's not a spider. That's a larvae making that stuff." I explained that the "stuff" was called "silk." We
then discussed why the children supposed the caterpillars were spinning
silk. Some knew a bit about spiders so they thought the larvae were making a web to catch things in. Others thought they might be making a bed
or house. Still others remembered some pictures I had shown them and a
video and understood that they spun the silk to make the anchor for the
chrysalis.

The last time I studied butterflies with the children, I had decided not
to spoil the excitement by telling them what was going to happen. I just
encouraged them to observe so they could discover the changes themselves. But then the changes happened so quickly, we missed a lot and
there was no way to go back and see it again. None of us actually saw the
transformations happening, so with this butterfly study, I made sure the
children (and I) knew what to expect. During group time, we read books
about monarch butterflies. We looked at photographs and mini-movies
of caterpillars changing to chrysalises. I talked to them about the *J* formation—how they hang and become like the letter *J* and then their skin
splits. I told them that the butterflies would lay eggs and then new tiny
larvae would hatch and grow and change just as ours had.

And if the children hadn't known what was expected, we might have
missed seeing the caterpillars turning into chrysalises. Ezra was the one
who first noticed it. He was looking in the butterfly garden when he

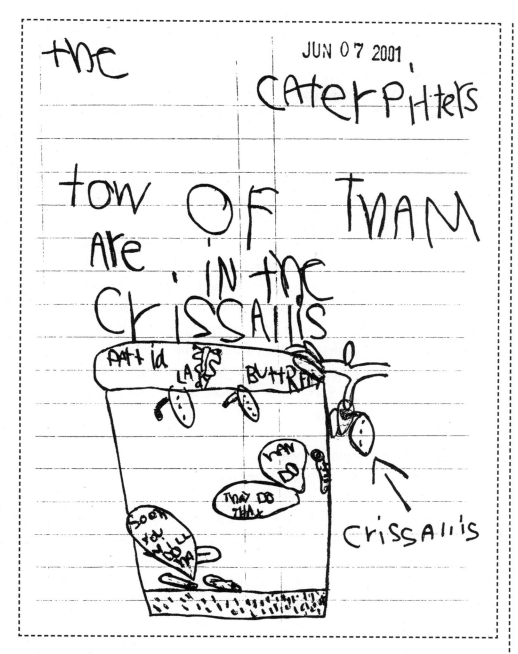

Figure 3–12 *A Page in the Big Book by Sonia, Age Five*

yelled out, "Hey, one of the caterpillars is doing a *J*!" and I ran and got a video camera so I could capture it on tape. It was quick—it all takes about a minute and half and I've never witnessed it before and neither had the children. There was just so much energy in the room, and all the children were talking at the same time about what they were seeing: "Wow, it's starting to wiggle." "It's dancing." "It's changing right now!"

"It's taking off its skin. It's getting out!" "Look, another one is shaking." "He's turning into a pupa, too."

It was just so neat because we could actually see the caterpillar's skin splitting. It's one thing to see a picture in a book; it's a totally different thing to get to see it happen firsthand. And because the children knew what to expect, they didn't panic, thinking that the butterflies were sick or dying. They knew this was normal, this is just what butterflies do. The children in my class wanted to see the tape again and again, and we showed it to another class too because theirs had turned overnight.

I asked the children to draw pictures of what they thought it looked like inside the pupae so I could understand what they were thinking. They really had no idea. Most tried to draw full-grown butterflies all folded up while a few drew a caterpillar with wings. And then we waited for the butterflies to emerge. And then on the thirteenth day, something happened. The pupae became transparent and we could see inside. We couldn't see any shapes, but we could see the butterflies' colors. And then the next day, it happened. It was like witnessing a birth. At first the butterflies looked like ants with wet, folded wings. And then we watched as these butterflies spread their wings.

The children were entranced. They would press their noses against the mesh, their eyes wide open, and look at those butterflies.

I took macro pictures of the butterflies, too, so that the children could see the butterflies' fur and eyes, and they were thrilled to see their proboscises, too. The children just loved that word *proboscis*—there's something empowering about knowing big words and understanding what these words mean. We even made up a song about the butterfly parts (including the proboscis, of course) that the children sang again and again, and later I found out that they taught it to their families, too.

We put a little dish of sugar water into the gardens so we could watch the butterflies for a couple of days. Most of the kids actually got a chance to see them use their proboscis. But after a few days, we let the butterflies go. We had had visiting animals before and the children understood that we could not keep the butterflies; they knew they needed to go out into their own environment. We all went outside to open the butterfly garden and say goodbye to the butterflies. Lyle said, "Go free little butterfly." Anna said, "There it goes. I didn't know how high it could fly. Above the trees."

Perhaps the most important outcome of this study was the excitement and fascination it generated in the children—the sense of wonder

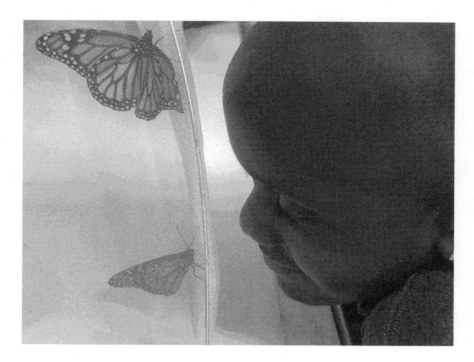

Figure 3–13

about the transformations they witnessed. But the children also were introduced to a life cycle different from their own: the development of an animal through metamorphosis.

From the start, Ms. Howard made an interesting decision, based on her own prior experience, to tell the children about the process of caterpillars turning into chrysalises before they had seen it. It is very important for young children to learn from their direct observations, but there are times, such as this one, when knowing what to expect can keep motivation high, focus observation on an event, and enrich the dialogue among children.

Given a focus on transformation from stage to stage over time, it is important to have many ways for making the process visible to children. In this class, the children had many opportunities to represent and record what was happening in the class book and the individual books. Ms. Howard referred to these records daily in conversation, reminding the children, for example, that those big fat striped caterpillars had once been little skinny green caterpillars, or that the caterpillars had shed their skin as they were pupating. Not all teachers will have a video and digital camera to work with but it is important to realize how powerful they are as teaching and learning tools. In this

Figure 3–14

case, a process that took just a few moments could be viewed over and over again, and the digital pictures could be used to make books and documentation panels and even to let the children take home. The Web and books offer beautiful resources for the children, but Ms. Howard's video and digital photos were of *their* monarch and thus real.

The children's enthusiasm was high and we were not ready to stop. Besides, I somehow wanted to pull it all together. These had been very exciting times. Throughout the butterfly study, I read the children a lot of scientific books about butterflies. I saved *The Very Hungry Caterpillar* for last. Before I read the book, I told the children that the author makes some mistakes, and it's their job to find out what they are. The children said, "Hey, caterpillars don't eat lollipops." "Butterflies don't have cocoons. They have chrysalises." And then Anna said, "He didn't talk about how the caterpillar pupated. [She really used the word!] He just went right from caterpillar to chrysalis." That was something I had never really noticed before, and I was amazed that she had picked up on the fact that the author had left out the entire process of change.

Then we took the stage idea a step further. First we reviewed the children's big book and the notebooks that several of the children had kept individually. Then we looked at all the pictures I had taken and the video. I also had a neat documentation panel that had some of my pictures and some of the children's that showed the changes we had just experienced. Then I put music on and I told the children we were going to act out the different stages of the butterfly's life cycle. We sat in a circle with four children in the middle. They acted out the butterfly story and I narrated. I began by saying, "Once upon a time there were four little eggs on a leaf and then the eggs started to hatch so they started to open up. And little caterpillars bit their way out of the eggs and crawled out. . . ." So I was telling the story and the children were prompting me, telling me what was supposed to happen next. And the children in the middle were moving around. Then I said that the caterpillars started to eat lots of milkweed leaves; they were very hungry.

That's when the children sitting in the circle pretended to feed leaves to the caterpillars in the middle. Then the children in the middle pretended to hang in a *J* position, and they started to wiggle and they pretended their skin started to split. When the children in the middle pretended to be chrysalises, I gave each of them a dowel with a beautiful iridescent ribbon attached, so that they could fly away when they became beautiful butterflies. Then the children sitting in the circle pretended they were flowers and the "butterflies" were drinking their nectar with their proboscis. I retold the story, with different actors in the middle. And eventually, the children took over, narrating the butterfly story. The children's narrations were descriptive, even poetic. One child even talked about how the butterflies' wings were wet and wrinkled, and the kids who were acting it out were totally with her.

The children's delight and interest in monarch development is clear from the descriptions. There is little doubt that the children would remember some of the exciting events. But teachers can reinforce big ideas, in this case, the stages in this life cycle and the flow from stage to stage. Ms. Howard wanted to help the children bring the whole experience together, especially given that the emergence of the butterfly and letting it go had been such a powerful moment. The dramatic rendering of the life cycle story was an experience in which all the children could participate. It also provided Ms. Howard with a vehicle to assess their understanding.

In the Classroom with Miss Scott ----------------------

Miss Scott is a Head Start teacher in a semi-urban working class neighborhood. She has a very diverse class of eighteen three- and four-year-old children who speak ten different languages. There are some small green areas around her center with an assortment of bushes and small trees.

Plants are an important part of the living environment, but they can be intrinsically less interesting to young children than animals, which move and have homes and eat and sleep just as the children do. For many children this age, there is still some question about whether plants are indeed alive and whether very large plants (for instance, trees) are really plants. Early childhood classrooms are often decorated with plants; children often plant seeds; and collections of leaves usually appear in the fall. Miss Scott did much more to enhance her children's science learning.

Plants were a constant theme throughout the year. Beyond sharing her enthusiasm with the children, Miss Scott had clear goals for the children. These included developing the children's understanding that plants are alive and helping them develop an awareness of the diversity of plants and some of the similarities and differences among them. She also wanted the children to become aware of the parts of the plants and some of the things they do; plants' needs and how they are met; and any patterns of growth and change that could be observed over the year. As in Ms. Howard's story, the children were engaged in close observation and recording, but the focus on trees, and specifically leaves, provided additional opportunities for comparing, sorting, and categorizing.

Just as in Ms. Howard's class, the children in Miss Scott's room spent a great deal of time exploring the outdoor environment outside the classroom, finding many kinds of plants, comparing and contrasting them, noticing what grew where. They also brought some plants indoors and made small terraria, and they grew plants indoors to see the cycle of germination, growth, and development. In the following pages, we have included only two episodes from this yearlong study of plants: the tree and a visit to the arboretum.

I decided to approach the study from a number of perspectives. This year we would study plants outside the classroom and follow a tree very closely, we would grow plants in the classroom, and we would go on a number of field trips. I really wanted the children to become aware of the plant life around them, in all its diversity, and how it changed over time. We started in the fall. We created a plant nursery in the classroom with a variety of plants. Some were bought, some were donated, and some we planted. The children's interest grew quickly, partly because they started to see changes in *their* plants, and partly because I got excited too.

The Tree

We began our tree study three weeks after school began. During the study, we went outside once a week to look at the big maple in the playground. We watched the leaves change from green to orange and yellow. And then we watched as the leaves fell and the trees became bare. Right from the start, the children drew pictures of the tree, and I took photographs. Each week, I took one picture of the tree from the same place and one picture of the lowest branch that the kids said looked like the letter *U* so the children could really see any change over time. These were mounted in order on a documentation panel with the date and a few of the children's words about how the tree and branch had changed. I eventually had a fall panel, a winter panel, and a spring panel.

The children looked at these a lot and we checked them before we went outside for our tree observation to remind ourselves of what we had seen and noticed before. We wondered about why changes were taking place and predicted whether we would see any new changes. And when we went out, sometimes with photographs in hand (thanks to my digital camera!) as well as the children's drawings, we compared how the tree had changed from one time to the next. The documentation was proof that changes were happening, changes that weren't evident on a day-to-day basis.

When the leaves started to change during the fall, the kids wanted to collect them and we did. I made sure that we collected leaves from our tree and from several other trees. I wanted to make sure the children would have opportunities to notice the differences up close. The kids sorted them in a lot of different ways—by color, by size, by the ones they liked best. I suggested to one group to try to sort by shape. That led us to a discussion about which trees had which shaped leaves. We had to go

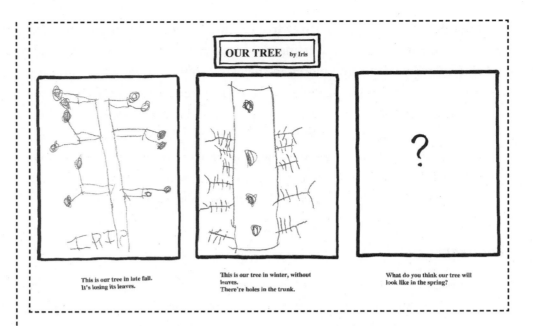

Figure 3–15 *Iris, age four, recorded her tree observations. Miss Scott used them to help children think about how a tree changes over time.*

back out and find leaves on trees that matched each shape. That experience helped the children to see that their tree had its own identifiable leaves and that that was true of other trees in our community. The kids were quite excited the day we walked to the next block and they found another maple tree with leaves just like their tree.

It was interesting when all the leaves had fallen (see Figure 3–18 on page 60). I overheard a couple of the children say that the tree was dead. So when we had a class discussion using our documentation panel, I shared the idea of the dead tree with the class. Then I asked, "So what do you think? Is the tree alive or is it dead?" The children debated. I'm not sure whether all of them really had considered the tree to be alive but most of them agreed that it was now dead. I think they were really working on this idea of whether trees—maybe all plants—are alive or not.

Spring was another story. We had been growing plants in the classroom. The children had seen seeds germinate and their beans appear and grow. But somehow they were really surprised when we found the first bud on our tree. We brought a small branch inside and put it in water so we could watch closely and draw what happened. The children were amazed! I reminded them of the discussion we had had about whether the tree was dead or not. There were some long discussions about the tree being alive again. I'm not sure whether they really thought it had died

Figure 3–16 *Five-Year-Old Amit Drawing a Leaf He Found*

Figure 3–17 *Children Recording Observations*

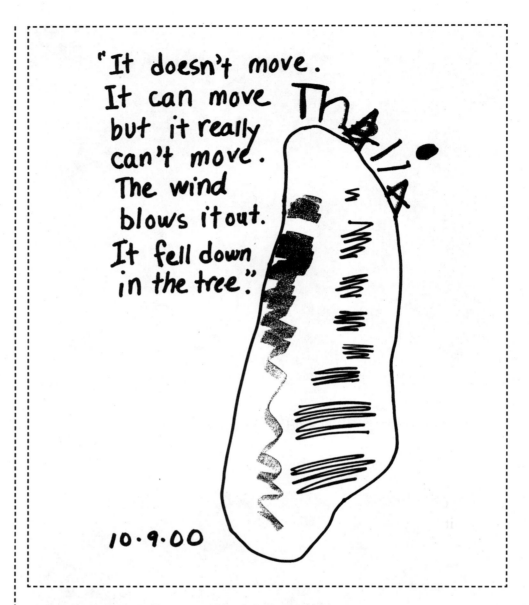

"It doesn't move.
It can move
but it really
can't move.
The wind
blows it out.
It fell down
in the tree."

Thalia

10·9·00

Figure 3–18 *A Falling Leaf by Thalia, Age Four*

during the winter but I do think that just about all the children had come to the idea that plants were alive, even if they didn't move, because they grow!

A striking part of this classroom study is the yearlong focus on plants. The focus on the tree and the regular visits throughout the year gave the children the opportunity to begin to see the pattern of seasonal changes and confront the question of whether their tree was alive or not and, specifically, whether it was dead when it had no leaves. Collecting and sorting leaves helped the children explore the concept of variation within a species—on their tree—and among maple trees, as well as bigger differences among other kinds of trees.

One of the dilemmas of studying plants with young children is the slowness of change. Not only does this impact children's ability to stay engaged, but it also makes it hard for them to track and think about changes over time. Miss Scott used her digital camera to great advantage here. Big copies of the weekly pictures of the tree mounted on panels provided a focus for discussion and made visible the change that was happening. The children could revisit what the tree had looked like at the beginning of school, at Halloween, and last week, and they could try to predict what they thought would be changed when they went outside next time. By taking smaller copies of photos outside, every child could compare the real thing directly with the photo. Although not detailed here, many of the children drew their own pictures as well, providing another link across the visits.

The Arboretum

By spring, the children had many experiences with a variety of plants indoors and outdoors near the school. Miss Scott also wanted them to look at plants and trees beyond their environment and see even more diversity of plant life as well as some basic similarities. That's when she decided it was time for a field trip to a nearby arboretum.

Before the trip, I visited the arboretum, taking notes about how the plants are similar and different from the plants and trees we had observed so I could help the children make comparisons. The water and swamp plants were really different, so I decided to spend most of the time there. I figured the children would notice the differences, but just in case, I wanted to be ready to point out the reeds, the water lilies, and the duck weed on the surface of the pond. I arranged for parent volunteers and for a bus. And I prepared the children. I told them that they were great naturalists and they had learned a lot by observing how plants and trees grow and change. Then I said that as naturalists, they were going to visit the arboretum, a place with lots of trees and plants. We talked about what they might see and what they might think about, like how the plants and trees were similar to the plants and trees we had observed and how they were different. I mentioned that I had seen some really interesting plants near the pond. Then I gave the children the naturalist kits they'd be using, which were complete with clipboards, paper, crayons, and magnifiers. As always, I brought my camera and the field guides. I also brought pictures of the trees in our yard.

When we got to the arboretum, we looked at the plants and trees and compared them with the ones we had observed—their shapes and sizes and the very different kinds of bark some of them had. Then Christina noticed the lily pads in the pond. At first, the kids thought they were leaves that had fallen off the trees, and they used sticks to bring the lily pads to shore so they could observe them more closely. That's when they realized that the lily pad had long stems and roots at the bottom! "Hey, it's got a stem." "I bet that thing at the bottom is a root." They just made the connection—the lily pads had many of the same parts as the bean seeds we had grown.

The children used the magnifiers to look more closely at the lily pad near the edge of the pond. They used the clipboards and paper to draw

"It's a lily pad. It's alive. It's soft. When I squish like this, it's not squished. It's not broked."

Figure 3–19 *Four-Year-Old Child's Drawing of a Lily Pad*

pictures of them.

One small group and I used the field guides to find pictures of lily pads and compared the lily pads in the pond with the lily pads in the pictures. Another group took out all the leaves they had collected and we compared the shapes of the lily pads to the leaves.

Several children wanted to bring the lily pads back to the classroom. I explained that we couldn't, that the arboretum was a place for naturalists and other visitors to enjoy looking at the plants. I did promise them that I'd buy a couple of water lily plants from the local nursery and bring them to school on Monday. We talked about how we could keep them alive in the classroom: "They'll need water," said one child. "We could make a pond," said another. The children were excited, thinking about the pond that we would create, as we headed for the bus.

And then Armin noticed twigs with small green leaves on the ground. Daphne wondered out loud, "I wonder where they came from." (Since we started our plant and tree study, the word *wonder* has become a regular part of children's vocabulary.) The children picked up the twigs and examined them. "Maybe they came from a bush," Ella said. We looked at the bushes, but the leaves were different. "Maybe they came from a tree," Tina said—and I can still see all my kids, with twigs in hand, all looking up the high branches. Naz was the one who saw that the leaves were like those on the oak tree. "Hey, they came from there!" And as we all looked up, we saw not only leaves, we also saw a squirrel, perched in the oak tree. We watched in silence, so we wouldn't scare the squirrel away. I looked at the squirrel, and then I looked at the kids. I was amazed at their ability to sustain their attention. Then they started to whisper: "What is he doing now?" "What's he doing with his paw?" "I think he's holding something." "He's holding a twig." "He's dropping it." "I think he's eating it!" "I wonder if there are any squirrels in our tree." For months the children had studied plants and trees. They had talked about them, measured their growth, drew pictures of them. They thought about how plants were similar and different. And they had watched them grow and change over time. This seemed like the beginning of a new idea— how animals use plants for their basic needs.

Focusing children's attention on the living world right around them is the main focus of life science for young children. But children's thinking can be broadened and their understanding deepened with occasional well-planned field trips to different environments. Miss Scott knew the children would see a wider diversity of plants than they had seen right around the center. She hoped this would help them to appreciate this diversity as well as some of the overarching similarities among different plants. The lily pads were a real bonus as they were so different and yet the children could see the same parts adapted to the watery environment. As often happens, the children surprised their teacher with their ability to make the connections between the structures of the lily pad and that of other plants they had studied.

The children's interest and focus on the environment led them to notice more and more of what was around them and to ask questions about what they saw. And as a result of their ongoing explorations and discussions, new ideas and questions emerged, namely, the interdependence of plants and animals. This topic will be the focus of their next investigation.

Summing Up

Ms. Howard's and Miss Scott's descriptions of their classrooms suggest that there are many ways to bring life science into young children's work and play. Although each chose a different focus—animals and plants—there are many similarities in how they approached their work. The basic tasks for teaching science are those described in Chapter One. Highlighted below are some strategies that each teacher used, which are particularly important to the study of life science.

- Both teachers had a clear focus for the children's inquiry, a set of concepts that guided their planning, and a structure for the curriculum. At the same time, they were open to the children's ideas and interests and the unforeseen.

- In both stories, the teachers used the local environment as the focus of the exploration. And both were aware of the importance of providing the children with other experiences that would broaden their understanding. Ms. Howard introduced the monarch and its marvelous transformation and Miss Scott took her students to an arboretum where they could see many different plants.

- Both teachers planned the study of living organisms to last the full year. This gave the children the opportunity to observe and explore many different organisms, building a broader base of experience from which to construct their ideas about living things. The year-long study also gave the children the opportunity to observe and think about change over time.

- Close observation was key in both stories, and both teachers focused on collecting and recording data through observation, drawings using paper and clipboards, noteboks, and class charts and books.

- Both teachers used science talks and informal discussion to encourage the children to share and clarify their thinking and as a way for the teachers to assess the children's understanding.

- The teachers recognized the challenge posed by the slowness of biological change and the tendency of young children to focus on the immediate. In both cases, documentation with photographs and video, as well as observational drawing by the children and the teachers, helped to keep the process visible for the children over weeks and, with the tree study, for the whole year.

CHAPTER 4

Physical Science in the Early Childhood Classroom

Physical science for young children involves direct exploration of objects, materials, and events of the nonliving world that surround children in their everyday lives. The focus of their explorations ranges from structures made of many kinds of materials, to things that move, to water and other liquids, to shadows and light, and to sounds. Physicists and advanced learners connect these phenomena by major theories (e.g., the particulate nature of matter), laws (e.g., Newton's laws of thermodynamics), and abstract concepts (e.g., energy). But for young children, the phenomena are quite discrete and interesting and challenging to explore. The theories, laws, and abstract concepts are best left to later schooling.

Physical science often is neglected in the early childhood classroom. Teachers, unsure of themselves, often view it as too complex for them and their children. In reality, children's exploration of objects, materials, and events goes on all the time, and physical science can become the focus of a great deal of their activity.

Doing Inquiry

Inquiry in physical science is very active. As opposed to living things, nonliving objects and materials can be acted upon. Children can manipulate them in different ways and observe what happens. They can repeat what they have done to see if the same thing happens each time. They can do simple experiments and investigations and collect data, draw their own conclusions, ask new questions, predict, and theorize.

In a classroom with carefully selected materials and the time and space to use them, children can pursue their ideas in quite independent ways in many contexts. They can use the phenomena and materials as part of their dramatic play and their games, as well as investigate what the materials can or cannot do. Physical science activity frequently involves making things and, thus, incorporates some of the skills of design technology. Children figure out how to build ramps for their rolling things, construct very tall towers, or create a flow of water from the water table to a bucket.

As in other sciences, children's inquiry in physical science also involves documentation and representation of their work, although the emphasis is less on observational drawing and more on recording important elements such as how the funnel was connected to a tube. Many of their explorations can lead to measurement, counting, and graphing. How long is the ramp? How far will a ball roll? How much water can fit in the container? How many blocks were used to make the tallest building? Children can draw and make models of what they have constructed, whether a water system with funnels and tubes or a drum that makes very low sounds. But representation also poses challenges in physical sciences. Because the focus is often on action, recording observations such as the flow of water or a ball rolling down a ramp can be difficult. Alternative media, such as photographs, video, and audiotape, can be powerful tools to record such events.

An exciting topic generates a lot of curiosity, and in a well-designed environment, children will pursue some of their questions and try out ideas. Physical science provides many opportunities for children to try things over and over again. Designing a ramp off of which cars don't fall can be a challenge, seeing how far a ball will roll down a ramp may need to be done more than once to be sure the measurement is right, and getting water into a baster can require serious effort. With teacher support, experiences such as these can help children develop patience, care, and persistence when things don't work as they want them to.

Physical science is also a vehicle for fostering children's understanding of the role of sharing, debate, and evidence. For example, when one child says her shadow puppet got bigger when she moved it closer to the screen and another says it got smaller, the teacher can encourage discussion. She can also emphasize that only through doing it again—returning to the evidence—can the children figure out what really happens.

Engaging with Content

The primary goal of physical science experiences for children is to allow them to explore objects, materials, and events in new and different ways. The more experiences they have, the more they can ask new questions and construct new theories about what is happening and how things work. Children will also raise many questions about how and why. Some questions such as "What will happen to the water if we get it to flow down this gutter?" lead to new investigations. Others may lead to simple experiments, for instance, "Which ball rolls the farthest after going down a ramp?" And still others can lead to interesting discussions or to books and other resources.

The raw materials for the study of physical science, such as water, sand, blocks, moving things, and musical instruments, are often present in the early childhood classroom. But it is the way they are used, what is added, and what is taken away that is key to the richness and breadth of children's physical science explorations. Adding different-sized balls to the block area and removing farm animals or hanging a sheet for shadows invites investigations that focus on physical science ideas. These and other examples from the classroom stories in this chapter highlight the importance of thoughtful choices by teachers.

Busy teachers may well turn their attention to other areas of the classroom when they see children's self-directed engagement with science materials such as blocks or water. But activity by itself is not enough: teachers need to observe children's activity and their dialogue, and they must get a glimpse into how children think about and explain the events they see. The better they understand children's thinking, the more opportunities they can find to extend their work and foster the development of more complex theories and understanding. They may present a challenge, help children to notice relationships or patterns of cause and effect, or encourage them to make reasoned connections between their experiences and their ideas of how and why things happen.

The content of physical science covers many aspects of the physical world. We have divided this section into three parts: Properties of Objects and Materials, Position and Motion of Objects, and Properties and Characteristics of Sound and Light. Each of the identified areas begins with a science explanation that suggests the level of understanding to be sought with young children as they explore the concepts.

Much of their thinking and understanding at this age is descriptive of things and events, but they also are eager to think about cause and effect, change, and transformation. After the description of each science area, there are notes on some of the conceptions young children are likely to hold, approaches they might take, and opportunities teachers can provide to challenge children as they encounter physical science in the classroom and in the world around them.

Properties of Objects and Materials

Developing an awareness of the physical properties of objects and materials is fundamental to later study of the properties of matter and how they change. In later grades, children will understand that under the appropriate conditions, a substance can exist in a solid, liquid, and gaseous state, and that these conditions are characteristic of the particular substance. But for young children, solids and liquids are quite different and, thus, we have divided Properties of Objects and Materials into two sections: Properties of Solids and Properties of Liquids.

Properties of Solids

Our world is full of things. Young children can be encouraged to use their senses and describe the properties of many things around them, including their color, size, shape, weight, texture, hardness, and flexibility. In some cases, they can begin to differentiate between properties that are true of the object itself (such as weight, shape, and size) and certain properties that are characteristic of the material(s) of which the object is made (such as hardness, color, or texture). Children also can use simple tools, such as a balance or a measuring stick, to measure some of the properties of objects, such as size and weight.

As children manipulate objects, they learn more about how they move, what happens when they drop, and whether they can stack one on top of the other. They may notice how some properties influence the behaviors of objects, such as how they move or what they sound like when tapped. They also can change objects, squishing a piece of clay or cutting paper into different shapes. Materials also change in special ways when they are mixed together, heated, or simply left to change over time.

Children begin to explore objects at an early age as they hit things and grab things and put them in their mouths. Very young children may focus on one or two salient features, such as the softness of the stuffed bunny or the stripes on the ball. Some details may attract their attention and others not. As they get older, they can be encouraged to focus on multiple properties of an object.

Teachers can create many opportunities to broaden and deepen children's awareness of the properties of objects and materials in conjunction with ongoing investigations in other areas of physical science, rather than in isolation. For example, when using different balls to explore the concept of motion, a teacher can raise questions such as "What are the differences in the balls you are rolling?" "What are the balls made of?" "Which kind of ball works best for rolling, throwing, or bouncing?" Such questions help children focus their attention on and discuss the important properties of objects and materials and some of the implications for their behaviors. In this case, children may begin to notice that some balls bounce higher or go a greater distance. By carefully describing the properties in each case, they might begin to draw conclusions and make predictions: the hard rubber balls bounce higher; the heavy billiard ball goes farther.

The exploration of life and earth science also provides many opportunities to focus on the properties of objects and materials. A study of plants might involve describing a collection of leaves; an exploration of earth materials might lead to describing the differences between the properties of sand and gravel. Children can also explore the properties and characteristics of materials in other areas of the classroom. The art area, full of collage materials, is rich in potential for discussing properties of different materials with questions such as "What is rough?" "What does tissue paper feel like?" "How strong is construction paper?" "What are pipe cleaners good for?" Similarly, cooking with children provides opportunities to talk about what they observe as they explore how ingredients change when stirred or baked.

Properties of Liquids

Children have experiences with many different liquids. They certainly are aware that liquids (such as shampoo, milk, and apple juice) differ in color, thickness, and taste, and children may have some sense that all liquids have some similar characteristics. But water is part of children's everyday experiences, whether they are taking a bath, drinking from a cup, jumping in a puddle, or standing in the rain. Playing at the water table, they can explore water and encounter some of the basic properties of a liquid: it flows and forms drops; it goes down unless made to go up; it takes the shape of its container; some objects float in it and some sink. Using water, children also can observe that when it is put in a cold place, it turns into ice, and when returned to warmth, it turns back into liquid water. It can even disappear.

Given the pervasiveness of their experiences with water, many young children will likely have ideas about causes and effects in certain recurring circumstances. For example, they will have floated things in water and may believe that only light things float, not yet understanding at this age the complex ideas of buoyancy and density. They may have figured out that when it gets cold, water freezes into ice, but they are unlikely to be able to explain how this happens. For other events such as evaporation, they may have interesting explanations or naive theories. For example, they may think that water disappears when left out in a dish because the dish absorbs it, or that clothes dry on the line because all of the water drips out, or that the water in puddles goes up to the clouds through invisible pipes.

There are many ways to provide children with extended opportunities to explore the properties and characteristics of water so that they have more experiences from which to reason. With carefully selected materials and teacher guidance, the classroom water table and other activity centers can become places to explore the science of water. Tubes and gutters encourage children's investigation of flow; containers of many sizes invite filling and emptying; small droppers focus attention on the drops themselves; and trying to float a variety of objects in a container of water can raise the complex issues of buoyancy and density. Children's investigations of water can also extend to the outdoors, where children can explore concepts of earth science, such as where puddles form after a rainstorm and how water runs down gutters, gullies, and streams.

In the Classroom with Ms. Diego ------------------------

Ms. Diego is a Head Start teacher in an urban district. Her classroom is in a public school. She has a class of seventeen four- and five-year-olds, many of whom have been in Head Start for a year already. In the story that follows, Ms. Diego describes how she facilitated an exploration of water over a period of several weeks.

Like many other teachers, Ms. Diego has a water table in her classroom that is open to the children during choice time. The children play in the water, filling and emptying containers and using it for dramatic play—to give the dolls baths, sail the toy boats, or "cook" a variety of meals. This story is about a water exploration during which Ms. Diego encouraged her children to think about some of the properties of water, how it moves, and how they could control that movement. It highlights the importance of teacher preparation through exploring the materials and learning about the science concepts. It emphasizes the important role of carefully selected materials in focusing children on the science of water. In addition, it offers examples of strategies that teachers can use to encourage children to reflect on their work.

Setting Up a Water Environment

In this first segment, Ms. Diego describes how she planned for the exploration, how she began the work with the children, and some of the "discoveries" that emerged from their work.

My children love to play with water. They love to stomp in puddles and make waves at the water table. And it seems like they could "wash their hands" for hours! I really wanted to capitalize on the children's fascination and help them explore the science of water. After reading a bit about liquids and their properties, I removed the boats and doll dishes and the water wheel from the water table so the children would really be able to focus on water flow. Then I carefully chose some new materials—containers, tubes, basters, and funnels—and I played and explored with some at the water table myself. I attached a funnel to clear tubing and experimented with different ways to move the water up, down, and around. I manipulated the tubes in different ways, trying to figure out how to make the water flow faster or slower, or stop altogether! Through my explorations, I was able to experience the phenomena the children would be experiencing. At the same time, my explorations really helped me to think about how I could help the children focus on how water moves and how we can affect water's movement. I also prepared my room. I set up one water table in the classroom with a shower curtain taped to the floor underneath it, towels to catch the "drips," and two big storage tubs in which the children could keep the new materials. My water table is small and only accommodates four children at a time. I really wanted to "saturate" the room with water play opportunities, so I got buckets and materials to make small water centers so more children could work at the same time. I hung up a clothesline for wet towels and our "water smocks" (which were kitchen bags with holes for the head and arms).

Then I prepared the kids. During a whole-group meeting, I told them they were going to be scientists. They wanted to know if that meant they were going to mix things. (Even at this young age, they have an image of a scientist as a wild chemist!) I explained that a scientist is someone who does experiments and makes discoveries, and as a class we were going to be experimenting with water and talking about our water discoveries. Then I had them close their eyes, and I put a drop of water on each child's palm. "How does it feel?" I asked them. Susan said it was slippery. Erica said it was wet. Yvan said it was sticky (I think he must have had leftover lunch on his hand!). Pilar said it was cold. Tyler said it was warm. Colin said it was cold and then warm. Then we talked about what they knew about water.

I introduced the children to the materials they'd be using at the water table, from basters to funnels to tubes, as well as the materials at two other centers—containers of water and droppers, small funnels, and small containers.

Then I explained that they'd be taking turns at the water table and the smaller water centers each day so everyone could get a turn. We also talked about the rules from wearing smocks, to mopping up spills, to being kind and respectful to the other scientists as they made their discoveries (see Figure 4–2 on page 75).

I purposely didn't show the children how to use the materials because I wanted them to figure out how for themselves. At first, I wasn't sure how the children would respond to these non-"toys," but I was pleasantly surprised at how inventive and engrossed the children were. One child, Teagan, held up a U-shaped tube and asked me, "How do I get water in it?" (See Figure 4–3 on page 75.) I turned the question right back

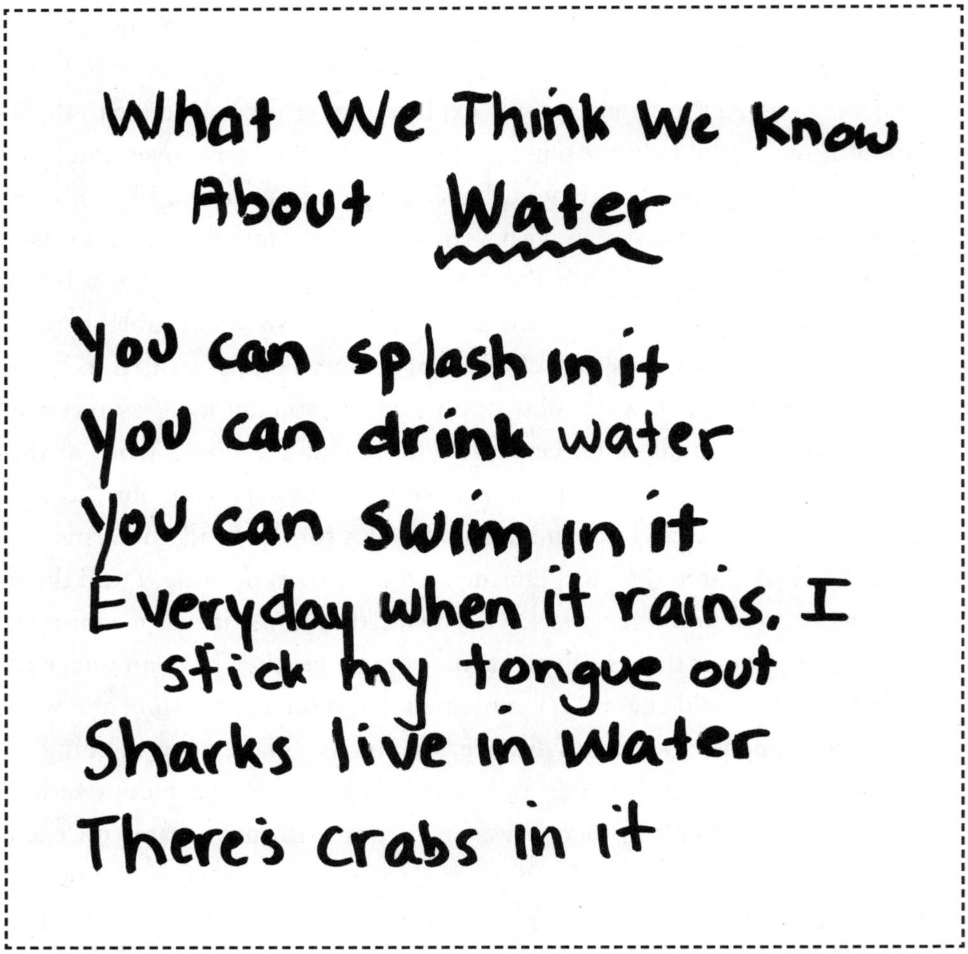

What We Think We Know About Water

You can splash in it
You can drink water
You can swim in it
Everyday when it rains, I
    stick my tongue out
Sharks live in water
There's crabs in it

Figure 4–1

at her and asked, "Hmmm, how will you get water in it? What do you think you could try?" She quickly began experimenting with different techniques. First she used a big cup, filled it with water, then tried to pour it into one end of the tube, but the tube was too narrow and all the water spilled down its sides.

Then she dunked the whole tube under water, holding the base, and that didn't work either. But she was persistent. This time she held up the U-shaped tube and used the smallest cup to pour water into one end of the tube until the water filled the U part of the tube! "Look," I said. "There's water in the tube! It's not coming out."

For several weeks, the children explored the science of water: how it flows, how to make it go in different ways (even up), and how to control

Rules for Water

1. Keep the water in the table.
2. Wear a smock.
3. Roll up your sleeves.
4. We can put our hands in the water.
5. No splashing.
6. Clean up the water.

Figure 4–2

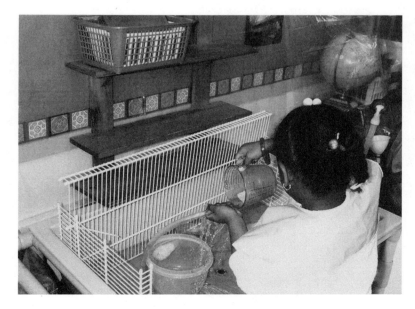

Figure 4–3 *"How do I get water in it?" Teagan asked.*

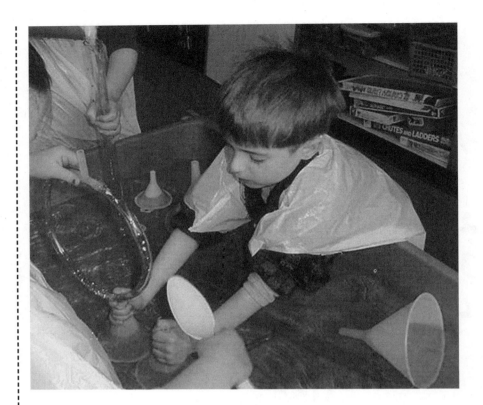

Figure 4–4 *Dinosaur Feet Walking Through Water*

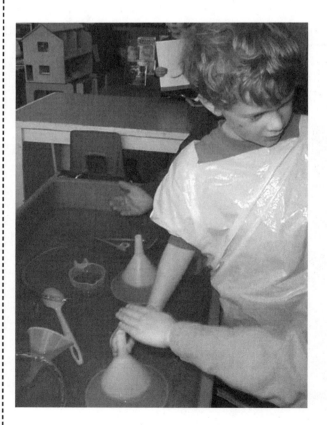

Figure 4–5 *"Can you feel the air come out the top?"*

it. They made whirlpools, used tubes to make water pathways, and experimented with funnels.

Colin was particularly fascinated by the effect of the funnels when he pushed them straight down, large end first, into the water as if they were dinosaur feet walking through water.

He noticed that when he pulled them out, "they kind of stuck." When I asked why that might have happened, Pilar suggested, "Maybe it's because there is a little part that sticks out a little further and it gets caught." Another child tried it and noticed that air came out of the small hole when he pushed the funnel down. He was excited then, saying, "Feel it, feel the air. You gotta feel the air." I asked why they thought that might happen. When they couldn't answer, we checked to see if there was any water inside of the funnel when it was under water, and there was. So I led them by saying, "So now water is taking up some of the space in the funnel. Where do you think the air that was in there has to go?" They all said, "Out the top!"

After about a week or so, I added some rigid tubes that could be capped at both ends so the children could continue looking at the relationship between air and water. I also added pumps so the children could explore how they could move water farther and faster.

Figure 4–6 *Making Whirlpools*

The kids were continually making new discoveries, and it seemed like every other minute someone was saying, "Look, I have another discovery," or "Come see my discovery." And each time, I headed to the water table with digital camera in hand to capture the discovery. The children then dictated what they did and what they discovered, and I attached their dictations to the photos for our class book called *Our Water Discoveries,* which we laminated and kept next to the water table.

As the children explored the water, we had weekly science talks where I invited the children to demonstrate a discovery that they made about water. Pilar demonstrated the way she added the magic ingredient to the pretend soup she'd been making at the water table. She showed us how she attached a funnel to a long piece of clear tubing, filled it with water, and moved the funnel up and down to control how much "magic ingredient" flowed into her soup. At another science talk, Brenda wanted to demonstrate the bubble she could make inside of a straight tube.

Figure 4–7 *A Water Discovery*

With a stopper on one end of the tube, she used a scoop to fill the tube with water. Then, she stopped the other end of the tube. She pretended she was presenting a magic trick, and she said, "As you can see, it is all full of water, right?" Then, she turned the tube around and we watched as a very smooth-looking bubble traveled up through the tube. "Whoa!" "That is so cool!" exclaimed the crowd. "What happened, Brenda?" I asked. She said that the "cap covers the very, very top." "What is in the very, very top?" I asked. The class exclaimed, "*Air!*" This discussion got us going on several more demonstrations that showed us that air "always wants to be at the top." The traveling air bubble experience was a perfect way to show that no matter which way you turn the tube (even if you hold it sideways and tip it back and forth), the air *always* wants to be on top. One of the other demonstrations included putting a turkey baster into the top of a tube that had water in it and watching the bubbles come to the top after we squeezed the baster.

Figure 4–8 *Brenda shows how she made a bubble in the tube.*

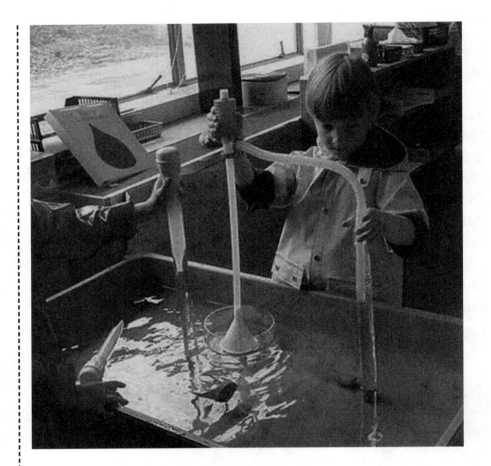

Figure 4–9 *How does a pump work?*

At one point, Kris noticed something about our water pump that I had not noticed myself. He saw the red "flap" inside the pump that went "up and down when you squeeze the ball." He tried it out to figure out when it went up and when it went down. "It goes up when you squeeze it, and then it goes down when you let go!" I asked him to explain this at a science talk. The class was absolutely glued to his demonstration. We were all huddled closely so that everyone could see the little red flap. Kris continued to explain his discovery, and I was thoroughly impressed by how well he understood the function of this contraption. He explained it better than I could have. He said, "When you squeeze the water *up*, it lifts up so that the water can get by, but when you are done squeezing, it goes down so that the water can't go back down that tube. Then it comes out this tube instead!" He really *got* it! And so did most of the others because of his skillful explanation.

Teagan asked me an interesting question after one of these talks: "When are we going to start learning about water?" Her question took me aback since we had been doing *so much* water learning. I said, "Oh, but Teagan, did you know that you have already learned *lots* about water just by experimenting with it? Remember all of the discoveries that we talked about and all of the cool things we can make the water do now that we didn't know about before?" She thought for a moment, then smiled.

Teagan's question made me realize the importance of making the children's learning visible. And as a result, I've started to do much more documenting of what the children are doing and learning, while sharing that documentation with the children.

At the same time, Teagan's question made me really think about what is science in the early childhood classroom. And it's not recitation of facts. Rather, science is about exploring and experimenting and discovering. And one more note . . . as I look back at some of these discoveries, it really hit me that the children are discovering just as much about *air* as about water; we're finding that the two go hand in hand.

Many teachers worry about whether they know enough science, particularly physical science, to guide children's inquiry. In this opening segment, Ms. Diego describes how she approached this concern by exploring water herself, using the same materials the children would use. By doing this, she was better able to focus the children's attention on interesting events, make suggestions, and guide their discoveries. It also helped clarify the science focus of the children's work.

Ms. Diego's story illustrates the importance of thinking carefully about what materials to offer and when to offer them. As in many classrooms, she had a water table, and the children had engaged with it in a variety of ways, primarily related to their dramatic play. Ms. Diego's first step was to temporarily replace the dolls and toys in the water table with flexible tubing, funnels, basters, and containers that would focus the children on the behavior of water. In this story, the children also became intrigued with air and its behavior in relation to the water, in particular, the idea that if there was air in a space, there could be no water. The rigid tubing and pumps, added later, extended this interest.

In other classrooms, the children brought other dramatic play contexts to their water play such as making magic potions or setting up a

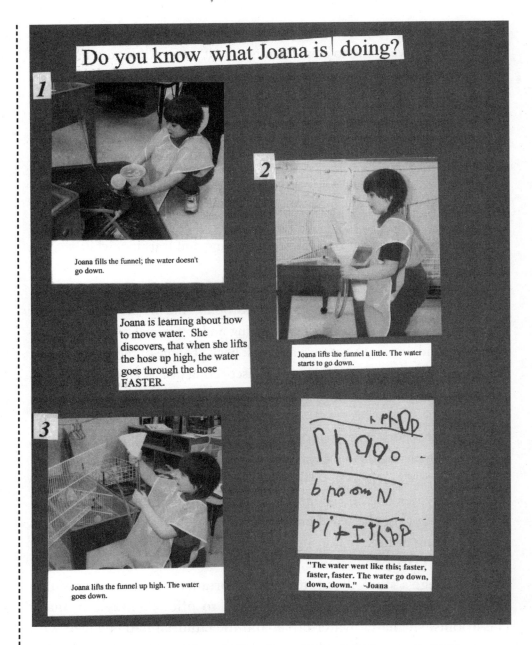

Do you know what Joana is doing?

1 Joana fills the funnel; the water doesn't go down.

Joana is learning about how to move water. She discovers, that when she lifts the hose up high, the water goes through the hose FASTER.

2 Joana lifts the funnel a little. The water starts to go down.

3 Joana lifts the funnel up high. The water goes down.

"The water went like this; faster, faster, faster. The water go down, down, down." -Joana

Figure 4–10 *Documenting What Four-Year-Old Joana Is Learning About Water*

lemonade machine. But here the play was mainly exploratory, with the focus on what the water was doing and how they could control it.

In an active science classroom, there is a great deal of interaction and talk among children and between teachers and children as they work. Teachers' words or actions can support and guide children's work. Ms. Diego's response to Teagan's "How do I get the water in it?" is a good example of how teachers can support a child's question by simply affirming it.

Putting their thoughts into words also helps children clarify and think about their own thinking. They can describe what they see, try to explain what they are doing, and predict what might happen. Ms. Diego provided the children with opportunities to share their ideas and reflect on their experiences by having regular large-group science talks. Teachers can use science talks to ask children to describe what they have seen and done and present their evidence and thoughts. They can encourage children to raise questions about one another's evidence and ideas, and connect their own work to that of others. Science talks also can encourage children to try something out that they have heard about or seen, thus extending their work in new directions.

"But when are we going to start learning about water?" Teagan wanted to know. Teagan's question may simply have reflected her equating learning with facts. Regardless of where it came from, it raises the importance of documenting the science work. For children to build on experiences from day to day and even week to week, teachers need to make the process and discoveries of children's work visible. Ms. Diego's class book, *Our Water Discoveries*, is one way. Documentation panels that feature children's work and ideas is another.

The Drops

The children's work at the water table over several weeks led to interesting discoveries about the movement of water. In this next segment, Ms. Diego describes the children's work at a water center, and how these experiences helped the children focus on the behavior of very small amounts of water—drops—what they look like, how they move, and what happens to them on different surfaces.

I set up a water center for the children to explore drops, how they are formed, and how they behave on different surfaces. I set out six trays, each with small droppers and jars of blue tinted water so the children would really be able to see the effects. I also included lots of different materials from wax paper to paper towels to dry sponges to sandpaper. During a large-group discussion, I introduced the different materials and asked the children to feel them and describe how they felt. Gabe said the sandpaper was scratchy. Amelia said the plastic plate was cool; Jeff said it was slippery, too. Brenda said the sponge was rough and the paper towel was fuzzy. Then I told them that over the next few weeks, they were all going to have a chance to explore drops of water and how they would "act" on each of the different materials.

Adding this new feature was a really positive step, bringing back some of the kids who started to lose interest in the water table. The drops also brought new kids on board, like Caleb. He lives with different foster families and has moved a lot. When he came into my classroom partway through the year, he didn't talk much. He'd say things like "please" and "thank you" and "excuse me," but that was about it. He just never got into the water table, maybe because it was just too busy.

But at the table with the droppers, he had his own space, and he had the freedom to explore without having to use his words. I'll always remember his little squeals of delight whenever he'd make a new discovery, whether it was figuring out how to make a really big drop or how he could make drops "capture" other drops.

Figure 4–11 *Caleb learns to use a dropper.*

Figure 4–12 *How many drops can we fit on a plastic plate?*

But before Caleb and the other children could discover anything about drops, they had to learn to make them! Initially, the kids just filled the droppers and then squirted out *all* the water at once; they just didn't know how to create one drop at a time. So I talked aloud as I demonstrated, and encouraged the children to try to do the same.

Figure 4–13 *How many drops can we fit on a penny?*

Figure 4–14 *Amelia and Erica explore drops on wax paper.*

Then I said, "I wonder how many drops you can fit on a plastic plate." First, some children tried to fill the upside-down bottom of the plastic plate.

Once they got good at this, I put some pennies on the trays. Gabe said, "Let's see how many drops we can fit on those," and the kids took on the challenge. (The kids were thrilled when they got fourteen drops on the surface of the penny without it overflowing.)

For a couple of weeks, the kids explored what happened when they put drops of water on different materials. The wax paper and the sponge had the most initial "draw" by far. One afternoon, Amelia and Erica were exploring putting drops on waxed paper. Amelia made the first discovery. She said, "It goes together and it stays together."

And she was right. The water drops clung together and even combined when they were next to one another. I asked her why she thought it stayed in a clump and didn't fall apart. She said, " 'Cause the paper is slippery so it just slides together." I wanted the children to compare the water's effect on different materials, so I asked how the drops would act on the sponge. After squirting a drop of water on the sponge, Gabe said, "Hey, it's different than the wax paper." I asked how it was different. Amelia jumped in, saying, "The drop sunk in." Caleb took a look and puffed out his cheeks to show that the sponge got all puffy. I asked them if the sponge was wet where he dropped the water. Gabe gave me this look, like "of course." "How about the waxed paper? Can you move the water drop so that we could feel if it made the paper wet?" He used the dropper to blow air on the drop and, sure enough, it moved to another spot. It was a very cool discovery to find that the paper didn't really feel wet!

Madison watched with fascination as her water drops spread throughout the paper towel.

She exclaimed with drama, "It goes, and goes, and goes, and *goes*!" Brenda, who was watching Caleb put drops on paper towels, explained, "It soaks in." I asked them why they thought it didn't soak into the plastic. They thought it had something to do with the plastic being slippery and the paper towel being soft. Madison also noticed that she could "spread out the bubble more on the sand paper because it's stickier" (unlike the wax paper or plastic plate). Gabe noticed that the drops on the wax paper "were the most still," while the drops on the paper towels were "the most spreadiest."

We had regular science talks during the time that the drop exploration was available. The children who had been working at the drop

Figure 4–15 *Madison, Age Five, Observing How Drops Spread on a Paper Towel*

table shared what they had learned about drops through their explorations and conversations. I was quite impressed by the words they used to describe what they had seen: *spreadiest* is my favorite so far! What a concrete and understandable way to describe most absorbent! During our final discussion, I brought one of the trays to the science talk and asked the children to share some of their ideas about why they thought the drops behaved as they did on wax paper, paper towel, and sand paper. Gabe, Caleb, Madison, and several other children all came up with ideas that had to do with the nature of the surface—its slipperiness, stickiness, roughness, etc.

I am continually struck by how the children can identify cause and effect and provide some beginning causal explanations that I used to think were out of their reach. With lots of experience and interactions with others, they can describe how things act, whether it's how a pump works, or how to lift a funnel attached to a tube full of water, or how drops behave on different surfaces.

Providing children with opportunities to explore water in multiple ways allows them to experience many different yet related characteristics and behaviors of water. Providing multiple contexts also allows different children to approach the material in their own way. For Caleb, the quiet, individual exploration allowed him to engage with the water in a safer way.

As in Ms. Howard's story about using a magnifier to look closely at living things, Ms. Diego also took time to help the children learn to use a tool, in this case, the dropper. Many of the children might have figured out how to use the dropper on their own, but by providing specific activities, she helped them practice controlling the dropper so that they could focus on the drops themselves.

This segment emphasizes the importance of teachers' interactions with children to guide them to go deeper. After Gabe had had the opportunity to explore drops on his own, Ms. Diego decided to pick up on his observation about the drop on the wax paper and ask him why he thought this was happening. Noting that he was thinking about the relationship between the surface and the drop's behavior, she suggested that he compare the behavior on wax paper with the behavior on paper towel. This brought others in the small group into the activity and included them in the reflection on the results. It also encouraged the children to describe what they were seeing and doing, building a descriptive vocabulary with words such as *stickiness*, *roughness*, and the wonderful *spreadiest*.

Once again, in this segment, a large-group science talk gently pushed the children to go beyond observation and description to come up with ideas or theories about what they observed. In this case, they were beginning to see the relationship between the nature of the different surfaces and the shape and behavior of the drops of water.

Position and Motion of Objects

Young children are intrigued with how things move, how to make them move, what makes them move, and when they move. Through their experiences, they are beginning to build an understanding that inanimate objects do not move on their own; they need to be pushed, pulled, or dropped to get started or to change the way they move. People can do the pushing and pulling, motors and engines can make things go, and things move when they are dropped or on a hill. Movement can be prevented as well. Barriers will keep a ball from going down a ramp, balanced blocks will keep a building from falling down, and a rough surface can stop a toy car from rolling. As they investigate, children can describe where things are and how they move and trace the movement of an object from one place to another. They also can move things in different ways and see that this movement depends on factors such as the kind of push or pull on the object, the shape of the object, the materials of which the object is made, and the kind of surface on which the object is moving.

As children explore movement, they also are building experiences about the force of gravity. They see that some things move by falling or sliding down a tipped surface. Different objects slide or roll differently on different surfaces at different angles. A structure will not stand unless carefully built with attention to balance and stability.

Fascination with motion begins at an early age. One of the first games a toddler plays is dropping something over the edge of a crib or high chair so that the adult nearby will pick it up. Other childhood games involve pushing, pulling, throwing toys, or building towers of blocks and knocking them down. Children also notice movement in their everyday lives when leaves blow in the wind, balloons float in the air, and cars drive by. From their experiences, they are likely to construct interesting theories about why and how things move.

There are many opportunities during the day for teachers to build on children's interest and focus their attention on motion. Outdoor play involves many things the children can move, such as balls, wagons, tricycles, and swings. A block corner that is stocked with ramplike materials such as long thin unit blocks, strips of heavy cardboard, and pieces of pipe insulation, along with many things that roll, can invite children to explore movement. A well-equipped block corner also allows children to experience the challenges of building structures that will not fall down and to notice what strategies seem important for building tall or wide.

Motorized and windup toys can add a level of complexity to children's explorations of motion, and discussions about what is making them move can extend children's discussion of animate and inanimate objects. The science of how things move through air is complex, but children can make and use kites, streamers, gliders, and parachutes. They can describe what happens, try out different designs, and think about the relationships among the movement of the object and its size, its shape, and the materials that make it up.

The following stories illustrate how two teachers used their blocks and a wide array of materials for explorations of the ideas of position and motion of objects. Ms. Chin's story focuses on ramps and rolling things; Mr. Jacobson's focuses on building structures. Like the water table, a block area is a common feature of most classrooms. It is a place where young children engage in a great deal of sociodramatic play and, through their play, become familiar with how the basic materials behave and "work." The two teachers used different strategies to focus the children on the science of the block area. In Ms. Chin's classroom, the introduction of the ramps provided the children with exciting challenges that replaced the dramatic play for the time being. In Mr. Jacobson's classroom, much of the work on structures was integrated into the children's dramatic themes.

In the Classroom with Ms. Chin

Ms. Chin is a teacher in an urban day care center. Her class is made up of sixteen children: half of them are three years old, the other half are four, and many are now in their second year in her classroom. She is fortunate to have quite a large space in the basement of a local church and, thus, has space for a large block area. This is very important to her, as she believes strongly that blocks have a central role in the early childhood environment and that children need both space and time to build and explore. In this segment, she describes how she used the blocks to help the children explore the behavior of different kinds of rolling things on many kinds of ramps.

Starting with Threes

My kids had done a lot of block building. They built roads for their cars and trucks to drive on, towers for their guys to fall off of—and it was the story that drove the play. I wanted to see if the children would respond to a change of focus to the movement of things on ramps. So one afternoon I brought a bunch of hollow wooden blocks outside along with some planks and several cars and trucks for some of my three-year-olds to explore. Jared announced, "I'm gonna make a tunnel." Initially, that wasn't my agenda (ramps were on my mind, not tunnels!), but Jared was so excited I went with it. Then at one point, with ramps still in mind, I said, "How about a road that goes down into the tunnel?" Frankie picked it up and laid a ramp flat on the ground next to the tunnel. "What do you think would happen if we put the truck on it?" I asked. Jared put the truck on the plank, and we all watched to see what would happen. "But I want it to move!" Jared said. He pushed it along the ramp and it stopped halfway to the tunnel. Then Mike lifted the plank so the truck rolled into the tunnel. "Can you fix the road so the truck goes into the tunnel, even if Mike isn't here to hold it up?" I asked. Frankie leaned the plank against a big waffle block. He put the other end next to the tunnel. When Mike put the truck on the plank, it sped down into the tunnel. The children squealed with delight: "Wow, that was fast. It went really far." "Wow, you guys made a ramp!" I said. "Now I'm wondering if you can make a ramp that will make the truck go so fast that it will speed ALL the

Figure 4–16 *Three-Year-Old Boys Making a Ramp*

way through your tunnel." Quickly the children went to work, meeting a number of obstacles.

I watched as the children experimented, offering comments if I noticed them getting too frustrated. I'd say things like, "I'm noticing that this is the spot that makes the trucks bounce off"—just enough information to help them move along in their problem solving. I wanted them to do this on their own as much as possible, but I didn't want to lose the focus on motion.

Dramatic play is often the context for children's work with blocks. Their focus is on building something that serves as the stage for enacting scenarios of many kinds. But with the focus on the dramatic play, children are less likely to pay attention to the challenges they are encountering as they build and are unlikely to want to stop and think about them. By taking a few blocks, ramps, and trucks outdoors, Ms. Chin created a mini-environment in which she thought the children would be more likely to explore how the trucks moved on the ramps. Jared's interest in tunnels was easily incorporated into Ms. Chin's goal.

One might ask whether Ms. Chin's intervention when the children were building the ramp was the right moment to intervene or not. Allowing children to struggle with something and to try different ways of making something work are important parts of science inquiry. But Ms. Chin wanted the focus for the children at that moment to be on the truck's motion on the ramp, not on the building of the ramp. By offering a few comments, Ms. Chin helped the children solve their problem more quickly. Had she wanted the focus to be more on building structures, she might have let them work on this problem for a longer time.

Steepness and Distance

The three-year-olds' work with ramps sparked an interest with the other children as well. In this segment of the story, Ms. Chin selects some new materials for the block area that are likely to engage the children in a more complex use of ramps and to lead to thinking about the relationships between the characteristics of the ramps they build and the motion of rolling objects.

A number of the other children saw the work of the little group of threes and started to make structures with ramps using the little cars and trucks. After a week or so, I wanted the whole class to have a chance to explore motion on ramps and different materials for making ramp systems. My goal was to focus the children's attention on the systems and how they could combine materials to make balls (and their cars and trucks, too) move in different ways, at different speeds, and along different pathways. I played with the trucks, balls, and ramps myself to get a sense for the possibilities and to review and clarify some of my own understanding. Then during one of our morning meetings, I showed the children some cardboard cylinders from wrapping paper (about four feet long) and long cardboard "gutters" (four feet by five inches) that I made by splitting a few of the cylinders. What I liked about the gutters was that the kids would have to figure out how to arrange them so they could control the balls and get them to go from one to the next without hitting a dead end. I also put out a bucket of balls. Next, I asked, "What do you think we could do with these materials?" One child said, "Make things for rolling balls down." "Yeah, let's do that," the other children piped in. I then posed a challenge—I asked if they could work together to build a system that would make the ball travel *all* the way across the room. So many children were interested in working on the challenge that we decided to form four groups of four children each to work together.

It was interesting to see how different children interacted with the materials and how they worked together. For the three-year-olds, it was mostly trial and error. They'd place the blocks one right next to the other,

Figure 4–17 *Building Ramps for Balls*

Figure 4–18 *How far can my ball go?*

not really noticing if a ball or truck would go through. Then, they'd roll the truck down the ramp, and if it hit a "stuck point," one of the kids would try rotating the block and they'd try and try again. It was different with the four-year-olds. With them, it wasn't just about trial and error. There was goal setting and planning and problem solving, and it was a collaborative process. They weren't just sharing materials; they were sharing ideas, and one idea would feed into another idea. They were always talking to each other—setting goals, identifying obstacles, and suggesting solutions: "We need to make the tunnel really, really long." "But the balls are flying off the sides." "We need to build up the sides." "No, let's use the gutter." "How about we tape it so it won't slip?" "Tape it to the rug so the balls won't fall down anymore." "And

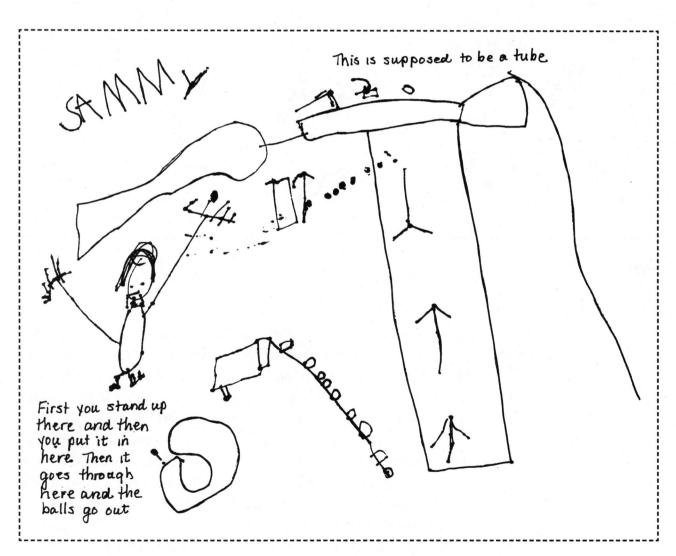

Figure 4–19a *Drawings by the Ramp Kids, Ages Four and Five*

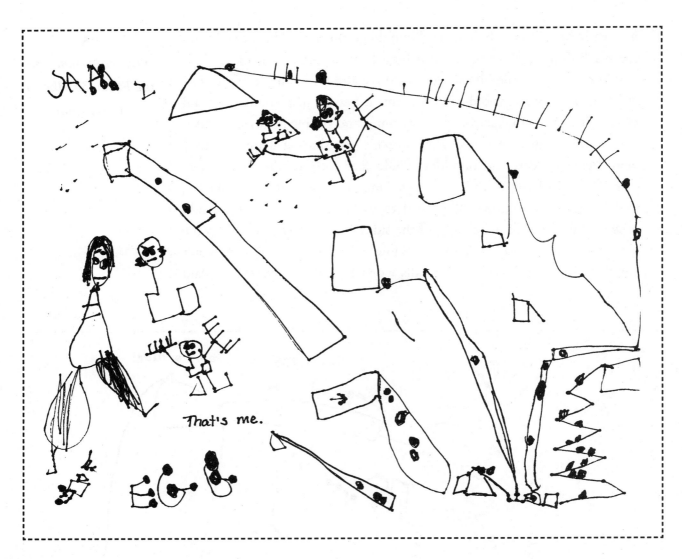

Figure 4–19b

put some blocks under the ramp to make it stronger." At one point, two groups worked together to create an enclosure with ramps coming from different sides, leading into long tubes. "Cool," shouted the children as the speeding ball disappeared into one of the long tubes and flew out the end. "It works! It works very fast. It works faster!"

I was thrilled by the children's constructions and their excitement about getting the ball to go through the tunnel, but I still wanted to focus their attention on how far the different balls would roll and what they thought caused any differences. So the next day I gave the "ramp kids" sheets of round stickers that they could stick to the carpet where the balls stopped so that they could explore how the height of the ramp and its steepness affected how far the ball would roll. I articulated the new chal-

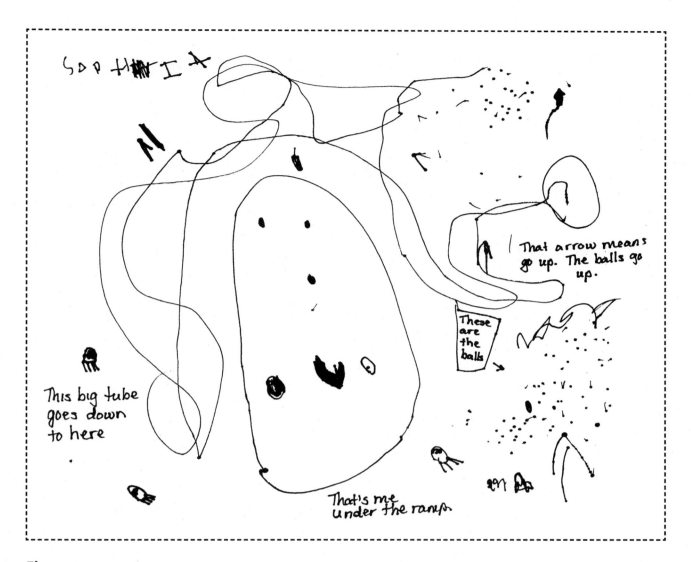

Figure 4–19c

lenge: "How far can you make the different balls go using the same ramp?" Not only were the stickers a source of motivation, but they also invited the children to collect data so that they'd have evidence about when balls go the farthest. I helped the little group design and use a chart to record their data. It had three columns. One had the name of the person who made the ramp; the next had the number of blocks holding up the ramp (one child just drew them). We used a yardstick and Unifix® cubes to measure the distance and wrote that down in the third column. The group couldn't have done this alone, but I really think the chart helped them think about what made a ball go farther.

We looked at the stickers on the floor and at the chart, wondering why sometimes the ball went really far, and sometimes it didn't. Fiona

You see the balls going down. This ball jumps down and falls off there and then goes back up. It jumps here and goes into there where the hole is Did you see the ball jump and go right into the hole? Look how many balls there are. That's the ship taking the balls to the next level.

The dots ∴ are balls

Figure 4–19d

said she made her ramp really high and her ball went really far. Jared said, "I did it this way," and he used his arm to show how he angled his plank. "How many blocks steep?" I asked. I helped him find his name on the chart. "Three," he said. Brendan had another idea. He had become a leader in the class since we started doing balls and ramps, and kids looked to him for solutions and to spark new ideas. Brendan said, "I made my ramp like a mountain. And if it's really steep, it makes the ball go really far and really fast, too." Then he had an idea for a new challenge. Could we hold the plank so that a ball would go down it really fast, then go up another plank?

Introducing new materials led to more complex and challenging work. The new kinds of ramps—tunnels and gutters—allowed the children to extend their roadways, and they also posed new design problems as they tried to keep the balls going. Some children created their own challenges with the new materials, as Brendan did when he suggested holding the plank so the ball would go down then up another plank. And Ms. Chin created challenges to help the children think about the relationship between the steepness of the ramp and how far the ball would go.

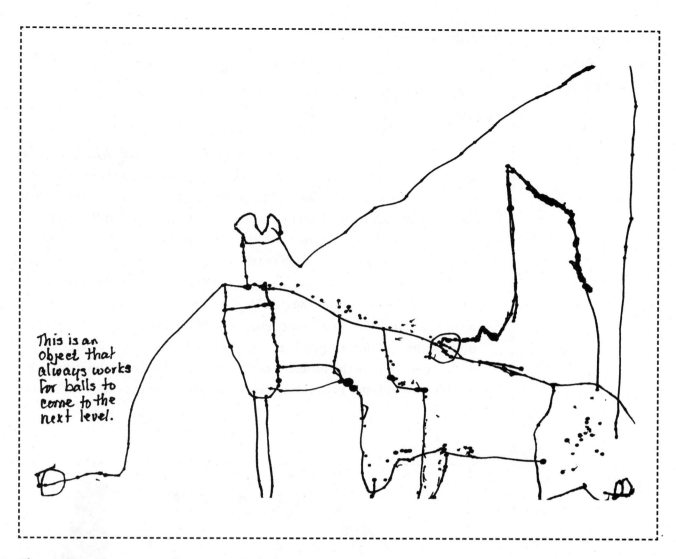

This is an object that always works for balls to come to the next level.

Figure 4–19e

Simple open-ended materials such as those used in this and other stories can be used in many ways and at many different levels of complexity depending on the age, challenges, strengths, and interests of a particular individual or group. In this case, the same materials were used by the threes to "try and try again" and the older fours to set up an experiment and collect and analyze data.

Ms. Chin encouraged a small group of children to collect and record data. The stickers on the rug provided a record of how far the balls went but not the relationship to how steep the ramp was. Both the chart and the measurement itself were challenging for this group of older fours, but it provided an opportunity for them to think about the evidence and come to the conclusion that "really steep" matters.

Marble Runs

In this last segment of Ms. Chin's story, she provides the children with an opportunity to extend the focus on how balls move on ramps by adding a new set of materials.

Whenever I give my children opportunities to compare materials, they learn more about each! So after the kids had been exploring balls and ramps for a few weeks, I wanted to give them a chance to use what they had learned, but with different materials. So I put out all different kinds of marble machines. There were the already-made machines, and the younger kids loved to just drop marbles in and watch them roll from one chute to another. Sometimes I'd say, "I wonder what would happen if we put something in besides the marble," and the kids would put in small beads, roundish pieces of plasticene; one child tried a grape. A few tried objects that would go nowhere—a tiny block and a paper clip. Then we'd compare how the different objects moved and think about why the marble moved faster than the grape or plasticene and even the beads. And

Figure 4–20a *Marble Machine by Matthew, Age Four*

we'd talk about why the paper clips and blocks went nowhere. The children decided that the "good rollers" were all really round and really smooth.

I also borrowed Duplo® sets so the children could make their own marble machines. What was so neat was that while the kids were building

Figure 4–20b *Marble Machine by Erin, Age Four*

their marble machines, some of them were making connections to what they had done before. It's not so much that they talked about their learning. Rather, I could see them using what they had learned. They'd say thinks like, "Let's make this really, really high so the marble goes really, really fast," and "We gotta make it steep too so the marble really pops up!" "We need something to catch them if they get away." The marble machine also reinforced what they learned in a visible way—that if the incline is really steep, the marbles can just fly.

Their discoveries and explorations didn't end in the classroom. At one point, I took a variety of balls and small blocks and other things outside, and a group of us worked at the slide in the playground. I asked them to find a really slow slider or a fast one and predict what would happen when we let go of it at the top of the slide. We talked about why they thought some things slid faster and slower. "It's because it's bumpy." "It's not slippery." "It will go really fast because it has wheels." "It'll get stuck because it's so heavy."

Then we sent different balls down the slide. I reminded them what we had done in the classroom and what we had learned about how far balls would go. Most remembered that when they made the steep ramp, the balls really went far. This time the ramp—the slide—couldn't be changed, so we focused on the balls themselves. "The soccer one will go the farthest." "No, it'll bounce." "I bet that little golf ball will win." "It'll be the superball, because it always goes far."

Marble machines are a common toy in early childhood classrooms and quite intriguing to many children. The younger ones enjoy watching and listening to the marbles run down the ramps. Older children also find them interesting, and often engage more when they can control the ramps. In this segment, Ms. Chin used the marble machines as a way to extend the work on ramps and rolling things by focusing on marble machines of many kinds. Highlighting them at this stage, after the children had explored with the more open-ended materials, meant that the children could bring to this experience a different level of thought and could construct new ideas about the way different objects move on ramps of different steepness, length, and material. Their comments suggest this is happening. The playground experience, using a variety of balls, extended the exploration even further.

In the Classroom with Mr. Jacobson

Mr. Jacobson is a teacher in a Head Start classroom in a small town. He has twenty children, ages four and five. He has always had a lively block area used by groups of children for a good part of the day all year long. In the story that follows, he describes how he reshaped the work in the block area over a period of several months to focus the children's attention on building itself, including the science concepts of stability and balance of forces, designs that make buildings stand up (or keep them from falling down), and the properties of different types of building materials.

Getting Started

Before we started our exploration of structures, I wanted to create an environment that set the stage for building. First, I took lots of photos of our school, capturing different details of the building, from the shapes of windows to the pattern of the brick walls. I also wanted to get the kids thinking about building, so I asked them to draw pictures of structures they'd want to build. Janine drew a picture of a castle. Manny drew a picture of a fort. Rico and Ben drew a picture together of a tower. Then as a group, we looked at all the materials in the block area and talked about what the perfect building space would look like and the kind of materials they'd want to add. They had lots of ideas. Ben said, "We need hard hats." Rachel said, "Nails. Screws." Becky said, "Oh, yeah sunglasses, in case it gets too sunny." Rico said, "And we need more space for our building."

So I got to work, expanding the size of the block area, carefully organizing the unit blocks and cardboard blocks and pieces of recycled foam so the children could easily access them and put them away. The Duplos® were put in the closet for safekeeping. To start with, I wanted the exploration to be about balance and stability and did not want any building materials available that stuck together. Hard hats and goggles were added to encourage dramatic play (and for safety), and there was a supply of different-sized paper and markers for representation. I put the pictures I had taken of our school building on the back wall of the block area, along with posters of all different kinds of structures from barns to castles to high rises. I thought the children's work would be less restricted if they worked in smaller groups so I decided to have no more than five in the area at one time. I also wanted to provide opportunities for more children in my class to build, so I created building centers around the room with small-scale building materials like cubes, small unit blocks, and KAPLA® blocks.

It's not that the children hadn't been into building all along. Even before we began the unit, the block area was one of the most popular areas in the classroom. But really focusing on the building itself was an adjustment for me and for the kids. Before, the children played in the block area independently. Practically the only times I'd get involved was when "fires" needed to be put out or when a child needed help engaging in the play of others.

This was going to be different. If I was to encourage a focus on the science of building, I had to learn how to be a part of the children's building explorations. At first, just setting aside time to be with them in the block area was a struggle. And it took awhile for me to feel OK with just sitting in the block area and watching. It's like, wait a minute. What am

Figure 4–21 *Building with Small Unit Blocks*

I doing? I'm not teaching. And what if the director walked in? It might look like I'm just taking a break, but it's so much more than that. While I was watching, I was paying attention to what the kids were doing and what they were exploring. Just "being there" was important for me and for the kids, too, helping them to realize the value that I placed on their work. But I also had to learn how to push their thinking without interfering with their plans. And their plans were driven by their dramatic play. Whether they were building with unit blocks or paper cups, their goal was not to figure out how to build a complex structure. Rather, their goal was to create a fort for their "guys" to hide in or a garage for their cars to park in. I tried asking a lot of questions like, "What do you think you could do to make this wall stronger or your building taller?" But they often didn't want to have anything to do with my questions; they were too intent on their play, so they just ignored me.

Our group meetings were really important in helping us transition into the science of blocks. Sometimes I'd introduce different kinds of blocks at a meeting, and we talked about them—whether they were hard or soft, their size and shape, what they could do with them. For instance, when I brought the foam blocks to the meeting, the children compared them with the other building materials they had used. They talked about how they were lighter than the wooden blocks, and they weren't as slippery, so they were easier to balance. And when I introduced the idea of building a strong structure, we experimented with the blocks as a group, thinking about how to make a structure tall but also strong enough to stay up.

The children then experimented with these ideas during choice time, and I spent time in the block area or at the building centers, observing what the children were doing and talking to them about the building decisions they made. Having talked about the actual building at meeting time, the children were more likely to want to talk about how they were building. I remember the time that Anna and Janine were building an intricate castle that stretched the length of the table. Anna was quite intent on balancing the rounded side of a half circle on the very top of her circle. Janine was quite sure that it wouldn't work and tried to convince Anna to "try a flatter shape." Anna persisted and, with careful adjustments, was successful. As their castle took shape, I asked them questions about the purpose of various sections of the castle, but mostly about why they chose the shapes and placements of the blocks. I watched both girls as they carefully adjusted and readjusted the placements of the support blocks. "This will make it not as tippy," Janine said. "Yeah, and we can put more on top!" Anna added. I asked, "Why couldn't you put more on top before you fixed these bottom blocks?" Janine responded, "Because it would crash, and we've worked very hard on our castle. Will you take a picture now?"

I had told the children I would take a picture when they felt they had done something important that needed to be saved. The pictures often became a part of a group discussion about building and sometimes became a bridge from one day to the next, helping the children to build on and extend their work.

This story highlights the role of the physical environment in children's science exploration. Here there is a large space for building with big blocks combined with multiple places for small-scale building to take place. There are photographs and pictures of familiar and unfamiliar structures, and tools and materials for representing structures in different ways. The materials available also play a large role in focusing attention on the key science ideas of stability and balance, as well as the relationship between the properties of the blocks and what they are good for. Materials, such as Duplos®, that stick together reduce the focus on balance and equilibrium. Foam blocks, with a very different surface texture and weight, increase the likelihood that children will think about how the properties of building materials matter when

Figure 4–22 *Anna and Janine's Castle*

building. KAPLAS® (small rectangular blocks, 4¼ inches by ¾ inch by ¼ inch) encourage a focus on design alone, without the added variable of multiple shapes.

Blocks and the block area are often places where children work on their own or in groups. Busy teachers are content to leave them be. An important part of what Mr. Jacobson did here was to become part of the building environment. As he described, it is not always an easy transition for teachers, from simply overseeing the block area to deciding on specific goals and becoming directly involved in the children's explorations. As he does so, Mr. Jacobson communicates the importance of their work, encourages and probes their thinking, all the while learning from what they do.

Photographs play an important role in this story. By taking pictures of structures in the neighborhood and putting them up in the block area, Mr. Jacobson encouraged the children to keep in mind the connections between their work and the larger world of structures outside the classroom. In most settings, buildings cannot be left up for long. By taking pictures of the children's buildings, there was a permanent record: something to talk about, to go back to, and to compare with new work.

Enclosures

Once the children had spent some time building with the materials that were available in a variety of ways and talking about their work, Mr. Jacobson decided to focus more specifically on one kind of structure—enclosures. He hoped this would focus the children's attention on the challenges of building strong walls and corners, as well as floors and roofs:

> When looking over the photos of different structures that some of the children had built, as well as at my notes, I realized that most of their structures were enclosures of some sort—buildings with walls and roofs (see Figure 4–23 on page 108). At the same time, I realized that through their many experiences, the children were beginning to build stronger and taller enclosures. I wanted to take it further, to help the children explore characteristics of various building materials and how different building designs affect how tall and how wide they can build.
>
> I had just read the class a story about woodland animals that make a home inside a little boy's mitten. Since the kids loved the book, I decided

to use the story to spin the idea of enclosures. I said, "The animals in the book needed a home that would keep them warm and safe." Then I showed the children our special Share Bear and said that she needed a home inside our classroom, and our job was to build her one.

So, with a collection of blocks at hand, we discussed how we might build a home for Share Bear. To get the conversation started, I asked them to remind me what they knew about building strong houses. Then, we began building as a group. Anna was concerned, though. What if the walls fell in on Share Bear? We talked about the need to make really strong walls to protect Share Bear. Jeff said we should lay the blocks flat on top of each other, then added, "Share Bear will be warmer that way." I asked him why. He answered, "Because the wall is thicker."

Then I asked what else we had to think about. Amaya said that Share Bear needed to have space, but would he fit? We constructed a cave for Share Bear, but Robin said that if he stood up, he would bump his head. I asked what he would bump his head on (we hadn't made a roof yet) and the children said, "Hey, he needs a roof so he doesn't get snowy!" So we used the long wooden blocks to make a roof and talked about how far apart the walls needed to be for the roof block to be secure. Share Bear got bopped on the head a few times in the process of

Figure 4-23 *A Four-Year-Old Making Strong Walls*

moving the walls around, but the cave was strong, and complete with a snowproof roof.

As we wrapped up the discussion, I said that we had made a great cave for Share Bear, but there were lots of other ways to build caves (see Figure 4–25 on page 110). Some children predicted that the foam blocks would be better for a cave because they were softer. Others said they could build a bigger cave so Share Bear could have more space inside. Then I invited the children to create their own caves for Share Bear in the block areas during activity time.

Since this discussion, the block area and the building centers around the room have been hot with cave building. The children have built caves with cardboard blocks, making lots of inside space so if Share Bear jumped, he wouldn't hit his head on the roof.

I asked one group using unit blocks about a roof. Some of the walls were tippy so I asked them what might happen if they put a roof on top of tippy blocks. So they aligned the blocks in the walls and placed the big wooden blocks across the top. Jeff surveyed the roof and wondered, "But what if the blocks fall? Share Bear will get hurt." They finally settled on

Figure 4–24 *Robin, Age Four, Building a Cave for Share Bear*

Figure 4–25 *Share Bear in His Cave*

using a big book for the roof, but they put a couple of square units on top of the book. "Why did you do that?" I wondered aloud. "So it doesn't blow off!" they answered.

Other children played out entire scenarios around the cave. Jeff and Yvon lined up an army of small dinosaurs that were heading Share Bear's way, saying, "Quick! The dinosaurs are coming! We have to finish before they come to eat him! Toot toot! That means they are getting closer! Hurry!" Working together, they timed it just right so that Share Bear had a slippery rock (arch-shaped block) below his cave so that when the dinosaurs arrived, they couldn't get up to Share Bear.

At first, the small blocks were not as popular, until one child created a miniature cave for a small plastic bear. My next challenge for them was to make a cave big enough for Share Bear out of small blocks! Because they would have to use a lot more blocks for the walls, they would have to think more about how the little blocks were stacked in the walls and how thick they needed to be to support a roof.

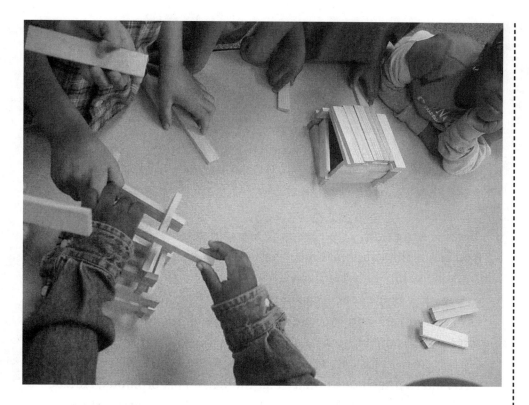

Figure 4-26 *Working Together to Make a Cave for a Small Bear*

This story about Share Bear illustrates how teachers can bring in science ideas while supporting and encouraging children's dramatic play. Particularly with building activities, children are likely to focus their work in dramatic contexts. They are less likely to build just to build; more likely they are building something specific for some purpose. In this case, the need for a cave for Share Bear provided a class context that worked and a task that was bound to lead to new building challenges. To meet the challenge, the children had to focus specifically on building strong walls that would support a roof. This led Jeff to decide to lay the blocks on their sides, and when he and Yvon were protecting against dinosaurs, to align them carefully. The focus on enclosure meant the children also had to think about how walls came together, how to create corners of some sort, and what do to about a roof. The materials of the roof had to be strong enough not to sag, but could not be so heavy that the walls were in danger. The many versions of caves using different materials and, eventually, different-sized bears provided opportunities to compare and contrast building materials, design, and scale.

Towers

Not all the children took on the challenge of building caves for Share Bear, although they did participate in science talks and small-group discussions, commenting on the work of others and sharing ideas of what Share Bear did or did not need. Some of the children were more into building towers, so that became the next challenge, exploring how to build them tall and strong at the same time. In this case, the construction itself was the context.

Before choice time, I simply said, "Some of you may want to see how tall you can make your buildings," and suddenly a group of children started building wildly tall skyscrapers.

As they built taller, some of them started comparing the sizes of their different towers, and we were into math. Elijah proudly announced, "My skyscraper is the biggest." I asked, "How do you know?" He said, "See, I used a lot of blocks!" Together, we counted twelve blocks. Then I said, "Amanda's tower looks pretty big, though." This prompted Amanda to count the number of the blocks in her tower. "I have eight," she said. Elijah said, "So mine is bigger!" "Can you draw pictures of your towers," I

Figure 4–27 *Balancing the Blocks to Make a Tall Tower*

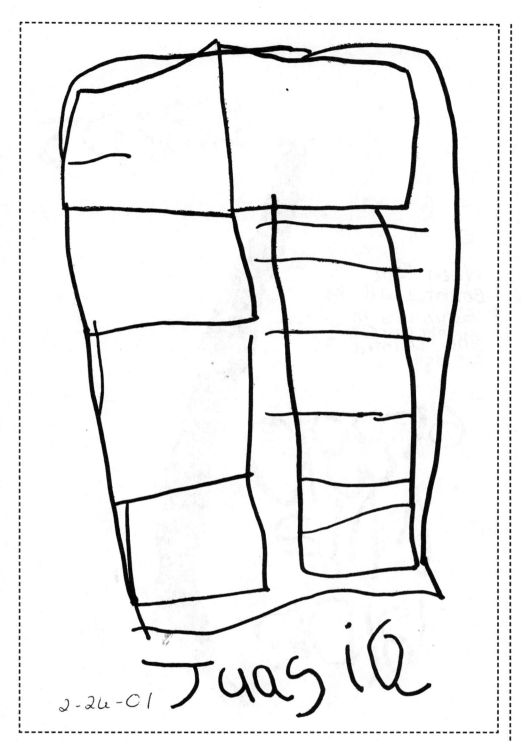

Figure 4–28a *Drawing of Building by Jessica, Age Four*

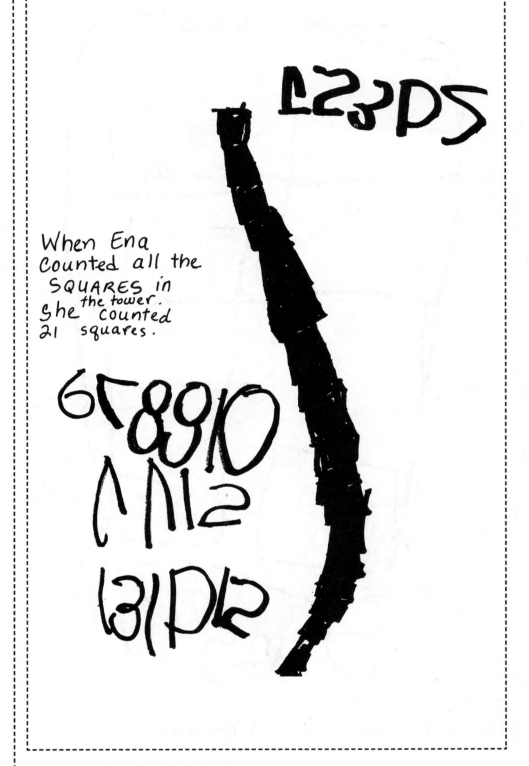

Figure 4–28b *Drawing of Building by Ena, Age Five*

Figure 4–29 *A Model of a Tower with Many Windows, by Lynne,
Age Four*

asked them, "so we can remember how big they are?" The kids then drew pictures, showing how many blocks they used in their towers. A couple of children used materials in the art center to make a model.

I tried to help them consider not only the number of blocks, but also the materials they used. I said, "Well, let's look more closely at the blocks you used." Together, we talked about the fact that Elijah used unit blocks and Amanda used cardboard blocks. "Are the blocks the same size?" I asked them. After comparing the unit blocks with the cardboard blocks, they concluded that the cardboard blocks were fatter. I probed some

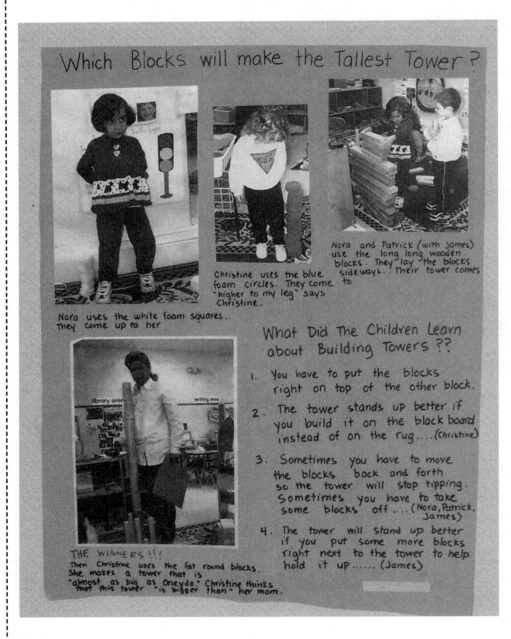

Which Blocks will make the Tallest Tower?

Nora uses the white foam squares. They come up to her

Christine uses the blue foam circles. They come to "higher to my leg" says Christine.

Nora and Patrick (with James) use the long long wooden blocks. They lay the blocks sideways. Their tower comes to

THE WINNERS!!!
Then Christine uses the fat round blocks. She makes a tower that is "almost as big as Oneyda." Christine thinks that this tower "is bigger than" her mom.

What Did The Children Learn about Building Towers ??

1. You have to put the blocks right on top of the other block.

2. The tower stands up better if you build it on the black board instead of on the rug....(Christine)

3. Sometimes you have to move the blocks back and forth so the tower will stop tipping. Sometimes you have to take some blocks off... (Nora, Patrick, James)

4. The tower will stand up better if you put some more blocks right next to the tower to help hold it up..... (James)

Figure 4–30

Figure 4–31 *Adding the Documentation Panel to the Block Area*

more: "So how do you think we can figure out which tower is taller?" Amanda stood next to her tower and used her hand to show that it came up to her nose. "Do mine now," said Elijah. Amanda stood next to Elijah's tower and used her hand to show that it came up to her mouth. "Mine is littler," Elijah said, looking a bit disappointed. I posed a challenge then, asking, "Do you think you could work together to make Elijah's tower even taller?" and they took off. For forty-five minutes straight, they worked together, trying to figure out how to make the tower taller and taller without it falling down.

Once the excitement of measuring the towers subsided, I wanted to focus in on what the children did to make their towers stable and strong. In the block area, I asked them about how they made the towers so tall. What was important to do? What would make their towers stronger? How could they make them bigger? I used the pictures that I took of their buildings and their own words to create a documentation panel about what they had learned about making tall towers. This panel became the

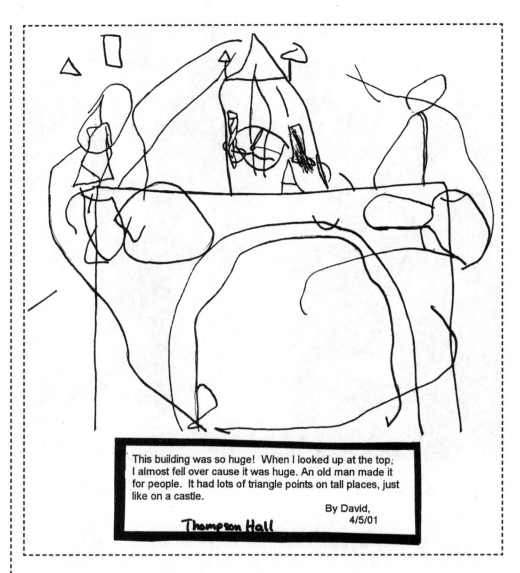

This building was so huge! When I looked up at the top, I almost fell over cause it was huge. An old man made it for people. It had lots of triangle points on tall places, just like on a castle.

By David, 4/5/01

Thompson Hall

Figure 4–32a *David's Drawing of Thompson Hall*

focus of our group discussion and then went up in the block area (see Figure 4–31 on page 117).

The challenge certainly worked to motivate some of the children, but after a couple of weeks, I wanted to get beyond building the tallest towers, so I decided it was time for a trip. It took a good week to organize, but the whole class took a bus trip to see a number of different towers in our town—several church steeples, a clock tower, a tall skinny building downtown, a house that had a turret on the top, and several more. For the trip, I brought a video camera and I got a bunch of disposable cameras and let each child take three pictures of parts of towers that interested them.

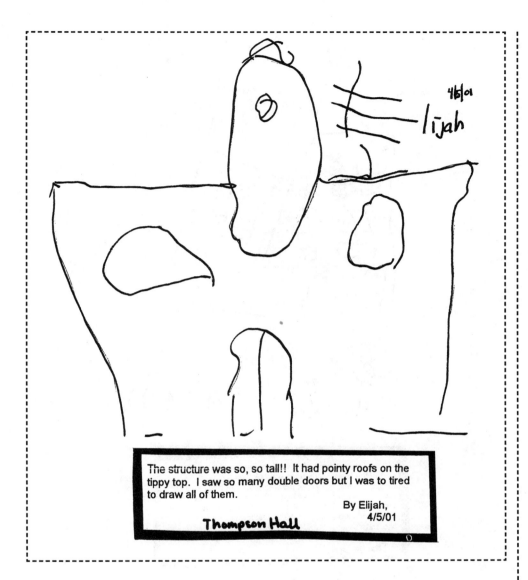

The structure was so, so tall!! It had pointy roofs on the tippy top. I saw so many double doors but I was to tired to draw all of them.

By Elijah,
4/5/01

Thompson Hall

Figure 4-32b *Elijah's Drawing of Thompson Hall*

After our trip, the children drew pictures of the towers they saw. They looked back at the photos they had taken and they looked at the videotape, too, to help them remember how tall the towers were and their different features—where there were arches, which buildings were more narrow at the top, how the bell tower was constructed.

The children began incorporating details of the towers into their own buildings. At the same time, they were really focusing on the structural aspects of building. They said things like, "Oh, I need to put a beam here because that'll keep it up," or "I need to lay the blocks this way to make it really strong."

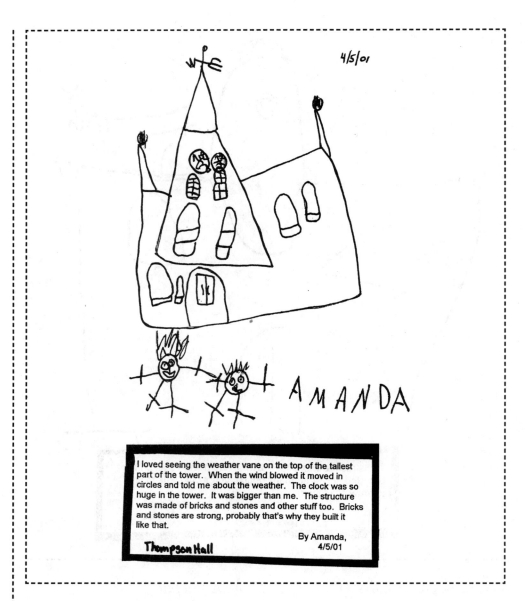

I loved seeing the weather vane on the top of the tallest part of the tower. When the wind blowed it moved in circles and told me about the weather. The clock was so huge in the tower. It was bigger than me. The structure was made of bricks and stones and other stuff too. Bricks and stones are strong, probably that's why they built it like that.

By Amanda,
4/5/01

Thompson Hall

Figure 4–32c *Amanda's Drawing of Thompson Hall*

Challenges such as this one can be a way to focus children on a very specific task and set of ideas. Setting the challenge of the tallest tower encouraged many of the children in the class to really struggle with how to build up and which blocks to use and how to stack them to make a stable tower that could keep going higher.

Comparing the towers helped the children consider how to describe the height of their structures. When the number of blocks didn't work, they had to find a different strategy—actual measurement. This example is one of many where mathematics, the language of science, is an integral part of children's work.

Figure 4–33 *"I need to lay the blocks this way to make it really strong."*

Specific challenges can become narrow and sometimes competitive when children focus only on making their tower taller than anyone else's. The trip to look at towers provided the motivation for the builders to make their towers more complicated by adding details that they noticed on the real buildings. Trips for specific purposes can also help children connect their ideas to the world outside the classroom.

The Architect

There are many connections between children's science exploration and the work of adults around them. Mr. Jacobson was fortunate to have an architect willing to come into the classroom.

I was talking to my assistant teacher about the children's structures—what they were building and the challenges they were facing. That's when she said she had a good friend, Phil, who was an architect; maybe he could talk to our class. I thought it was a terrific idea to bring someone in who could help the kids think about the steps people take to "dream a house," then turn it into a reality. And the timing seemed right. After all, they had been building for weeks. They were ready for a new experience.

That night I called Phil, the architect, and we came up with a plan for his visit. He'd ask the children for ideas for the perfect house. Then he'd use their ideas and his drawing tools to make a blueprint. We talked about what tools he'd be using—a square, a compass. Before his visit I bought a couple of examples of each tool to give the children a chance to touch them and play with them before Phil came in. The day before the visit, I brought the kids together in a circle and told them that we were

Figure 4–34

going to have a guest visitor who was an architect. Then I explained that architects draw blueprints—pictures of structures so that builders know how to build them.

When Phil arrived he showed the children a blueprint. Then he told the children that they were going to make their own blueprint of their dream house, but first they had to come up with some ideas about the different parts of the house and what each would look like. There were lots of ideas. Abby wanted a house with a balcony. Elijah wanted a skyscraper. Asa wanted a castle.

Phil kept honing in on the specifics, asking the kids what parts of those buildings they wanted. He sketched on the chalkboard, incorporating features that the children had requested, like Abby's balcony and Asa's castlelike arches. Meanwhile, he kept pressing for more details. "Should we have windows? What kind? What shape should they be? Should they go up and down or should they swing open? How many doors should we have?"

Phil used the children's ideas to refine his sketch, and believe me, my kids didn't hold back from providing Phil with feedback each step of the way. They'd say, "No the tower should be taller. You need an arch. Make a pillar. The window has to be bigger and round on top." As the children provided feedback, Phil erased different parts, then tried to capture the details the children wanted.

When the sketch finally passed muster, Phil began to transform the sketch into a blueprint, talking through the process each step of the way. He said things like, "I'm going to use the drawing compass to make the arch. . . . Now I'm using the square to make the windows that swing open. . . . Remember, I've been using these tools for a long time, and it takes practice. So just be patient when you're using your tools."

Because my group already had experiences building, they were able to share some of their own ideas and questions with Phil. Amanda described the building process she used, and some of the problems she experienced. She told Phil, "It was hard to build a really tall skyscraper because it would fall a lot." Phil asked, "What did you do to make it stop falling?" Amanda didn't take long to answer, "I found big fat blocks. I put them on the bottom. They're strong." Asa tried really hard to explain at what point his building would just collapse; he just couldn't find the words. But he didn't give up. Instead he grabbed a bunch of blocks so he could demonstrate. Phil and the kids started experimenting then. They built on soft surfaces, then on hard surfaces, and they talked about which surfaces provided a better foundation and why. They also experimented with different types of blocks and talked about why the bigger, wider blocks on the bottom helped to balance the structure on top. Phil was with us for an hour. I never would have predicted that the group would stay engaged for so long. But except for a few of the younger ones, they were with him the whole time.

Before Phil's visit, none of the children ever thought about drawing their plans—they just built. But things changed. We added a new step to our building process: making blueprints. That was important because I really wanted the children to think through what they wanted to build, what it would look like, and what features it would have. To encourage the children to draw blueprints, I put a table next to the block area with paper and drawing tools so they always had access to them. Not all the children were able or interested in doing this, but most gave it a try.

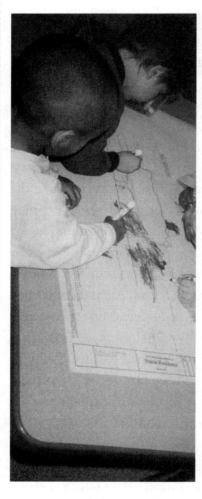

Figure 4–35 *Making a Blueprint, James and Charles, Age Four*

Figure 4–36 *Child's Blueprint and Building, Age Five*

Young children's work is usually immediate, each step guided by what came before. When working with materials such as blocks, their approach is often characterized by trial and error, and it is often difficult to plan. But in this story, the children had done a lot of building, had drawn their buildings, and had talked about how they were built. Phil's visit provided the children with the motivation, support, and tools to become planners. In this way, the children were developing a very important inquiry skill.

Bringing in community people or experts can enrich children's experiences and extend their work. It also connects what children do to people outside the classroom walls. Finding the right expert, one who can share his or her ideas in ways that are accessible to young children, is critical. Bringing in the experts also requires preparation, of the expert as well as the children. In this case, the children's work building structures meant they had thought about some of the problems and ways they wanted to build things. Mr. Jacobson also had discussions with the children about the visit beforehand, helping them to connect their work with that of an architect, while giving them the opportunity to use the tools he would bring.

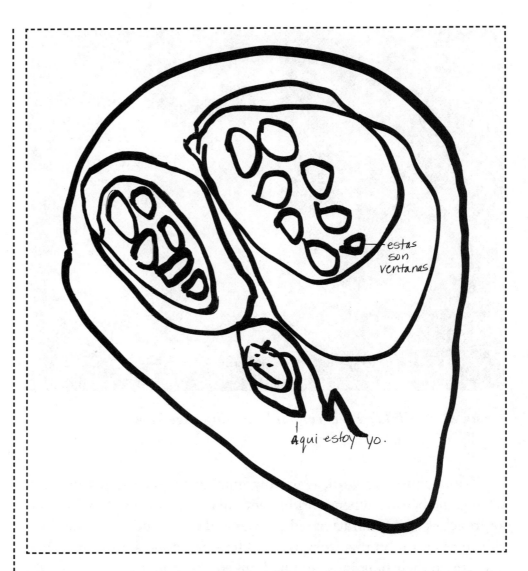

Figure 4–37 *These are windows and here I am. Valentina, age three and a half.*

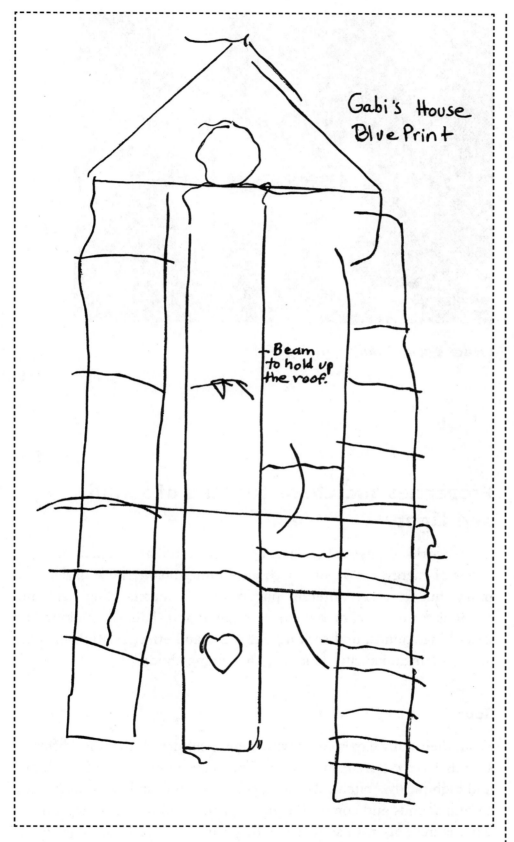

Figure 4–38a *Gabi used architect tools to make his blueprint.*

Figure 4–38b *Gabi's Building*

Properties and Characteristics of Sound and Light

In the world of physical science, light and sound are related: both are forms of energy. However, for young children, light and sound are familiar but are very different phenomena. Understanding light and sound is for later years, but exploring light and shadows, making and describing sounds, and seeking out cause-and-effect relationships are appropriate and exciting inquiries for young children.

Sound

From their daily experiences with sound, children know that different sounds have different properties. They can be loud or soft (volume) and high or low (pitch). As they explore sounds, children can identify certain sounds and come to realize that the kind of sound depends on what is making it. In some cases they can see or feel the thing that is making the sound (for instance, the string on the guitar) move back and forth, preparing them for understanding the role of vibration in making sounds.

Sounds are everywhere in children's lives. Children hear sounds from many sources and make many sounds themselves. They sing, speak, yell, and laugh. They make sounds for their toy animals and the front loader; they bang the lids of pots together and experiment with the piano, guitar, or other instruments that are available. But many sounds around them are disconnected visibly from their sources. Music comes from CDs and television and is often part of the early childhood classroom; the sounds of air-conditioning and heating and plumbing systems are steady background noise; traffic noises become a blur undistinguishable from the sounds of individual cars. To develop a deeper and broader experience with sound, children need many opportunities to make and explore sounds, their sources, and their characteristics.

As children study sound, they can listen carefully and try to describe the sounds they hear and what is making them. For example, they can listen for sounds in the neighborhood and try to find their source; teachers can make tapes of mystery sounds for the children to describe and identify; or with teacher guidance, children can create a "band" with homemade instruments. Children may notice the movement of a drumhead, string, or rubber band when it is plucked or hit, but that is not the primary focus of their exploration. Rather, the principal focus is the type of sound that different objects make and how children can control the volume and sometimes the pitch. Guided discussion can help children describe sound and develop ideas about the relationship between the nature of the sound and the object that is making it.

Light

Children have no lack of experiences with light and dark, and they know that light allows them to see things. Through new experiences, they can focus on different sources of light and how light can be brighter or dimmer depending on its source and how far away it is. They can begin to realize that light can make shadows and that shadows change size and shape depending on the location of the object and the light source.

At a young age, children are still likely to believe that the objects they can see contain their own light sources. Many believe that their own shadows are somehow separate from them, following them about in sometimes scary ways. Varied experiences indoors and outdoors with light and shadow will develop the experiential foundation for later learning of more abstract concepts of light as energy, how it travels, and how it is absorbed, reflected, or refracted.

Exploring light and shadows helps children develop new awareness and ideas about light. For example, children can draw their shadows on the sidewalk during the day and see changes. Flashlights in a dimly lit room can encourage children to think about the relationship between the light source and where in the room they see the light. Putting colored gels in front of a light source or looking through them makes the world turn red or blue. A light source, interesting objects, and a simple screen provide opportunities for children to notice that position and distance matter when they are trying to make a shadow of an object.

In the Classroom with Ms. Tomas ----------------------

The story that follows is about shadows. Ms. Tomas describes a part of the study of shadows she did with her eighteen children, ranging in age from three to five. Ms. Tomas' day care center offers a sliding fee and most of the children are dropped off by family members who work in the office building next door. Ms. Tomas noticed that her children were intrigued with shadows. But she knew that for the children to explore some of the science of shadows, they would need more opportunities to work with shadows in different ways. In the following segments, Ms. Tomas helps her children think about what a shadow is and the relationship between the object, the way it is held, and the shadow it casts. She also provides the children with opportunities to think about how a shadow changes when it is moved closer to or farther from a light, and what happens when the light itself moves.

Starting Outdoors: A Teachable Moment

We had created our own garden right outside our backdoor. It was Colin who first started noticing the shadows because we had talked about the

What Is a Shadow?

Everyone can see their shadow (Louisa).

It follows you (Ben).

The sunlight makes it happen because it's so bright (Costanza).

Shadows go away in the night (Lei-Anne).

Sometimes you see shadows in the night (Jeff).

Figure 4–39

garden needing sunlight. We were outside in the early afternoon and we could actually see a crisp line gradually crawl over the garden. "Look, a shadow," he said, pointing. I said, "Wow, you're right." Then I asked the children, "What do you think a shadow is anyway?" They had lots of ideas. Louisa said, "Everyone can see their shadow." Ben said, "It follows you." Costanza said, "The sunlight makes it happen because it's so bright." Lei-Anne said, "Shadows go away in the night," but Jeff disagreed. He said, "Uh-uh—sometimes you can see them." I wrote down their ideas and hung them up in the classroom, so we could revisit them later.

The next time we were outdoors, a group of children started playing with their shadows, running away from them, jumping, waving their arms to see the shadows wave. For a number of children, making castles

131

and birthday cakes in the sandbox was replaced by shadow play—seeing how many times they could step on each other's shadow or have their shadows touch hands (without the kids actually touching hands). Some discovered that they could make monster shadows, too, with four legs and four arms and antenna. Initially, the younger ones, in particular, seemed to be convinced that their shadows were always there—that they were really a part of them. But seeing their shadows actually disappear when they ran into the shade made them wonder.

Given their interest, I decided that we would explore shadows more deeply, focusing on how shadows change and what makes them change. On a sunny day, I traced several children's shadows on big poster paper at different times throughout the day—almost like we were making a human sundial. A few of the older ones were able to trace each other's. At the end of the day, I encouraged them to compare how their body tracings were alike and how they were different. "There's my head and my hands and my feet," said Costanza, pointing to the different parts of her body on all the shadow tracings. "And does your shadow change?" I asked. Karen studied the progression of her shadow tracings. "This one is big," she said, pointing to her morning shadow. "This one is more littler," she said, pointing to her lunchtime shadow. "And now I'm big again," she said pointing to her afternoon shadow. "Oh," I said, "so it's the size that changes." Over the next week or so, this group and others would come up and say, "Ms. Tomas, let's go out and see our lunchtime shadow." "I want to go measure my after-lunch shadow." Many of the children began to realize that the size of their shadows changed, depending on the time of the day.

This study of shadows emerged from a "teachable moment," demonstrating the reality that children are surrounded by interesting science phenomena that may spark their interest at any time. Sometimes teachers' responses to a child's interest may be an encouraging word, a discussion, or support for the child in some ongoing activity. But sometimes, as in this case, teachers make the decision that there is something valuable to be explored more deeply by the whole class. Given children's interest in shadows, and the fact that they can be explored in a number of ways, Ms. Tomas chose shadows as a focus—to help the children think about what shadows are, how they change, and what makes them change.

There are many shadow activities that can engage young children. Ms. Tomas decided to first trace the children's shadows to emphasize that shadows change. As the children compared their shadows at different times of the day, it was clear to some that they had changed in size, which provided a springboard for talking and thinking about what was different and what might have caused the change.

Moving Shadows Indoors: Shadow Theater

The next step in Ms. Tomas' exploration of shadows was to focus the children on ways they could manipulate the shadows and make them change. The outdoor work had roused their interest and would certainly continue on sunny days, but she felt a more controlled environment indoors would allow them to take their experience further and begin to see some of the relationships between how light is blocked and the shadow that is produced.

I have a wonderful book called *Shadow Night* by Kay Chorao. It's a story about a little boy who is afraid of the monsters that he sees in the nighttime shadows. His parents comfort him, while showing him he can make his own shadows as well. I hung a sheet in front of the window so the children could make upright shadows with their bodies and see how they could make them change (see Figure 4–40 on page 134).

In the meantime, I was thinking about where to go next and how to extend the children's investigation of shadows even further. I wanted them to really focus on making different shapes with shadows and how to make shadows bigger and smaller. The "post office" in our dramatic play corner that I had made from a huge, sturdy cardboard box was transformed into our very own shadow theater! The first thing I did was stretch a screen of lightweight fabric across the opening of the box (where the post office clerks once stood). Then I placed a light in the back of our theater.

During our morning meeting, I introduced the shadow theater. I told the children that they had already learned a lot about shadows by exploring them outside and with the sheet. They would now have a chance to learn even more by exploring shadows with real lights. "This is our new shadow theater," I said. "What do you think we can do with it?" I asked. Andrew said, "Make spiders!" "What else?" I asked. "Make a fat goose," said Costanza. "So you can make animals," I said. "Also look at this." I had borrowed shadow puppets from the classroom next door—they were beautiful, with bright colors on parchment paper, and my assistant teacher and I put on a little puppet show. The kids were so excited.

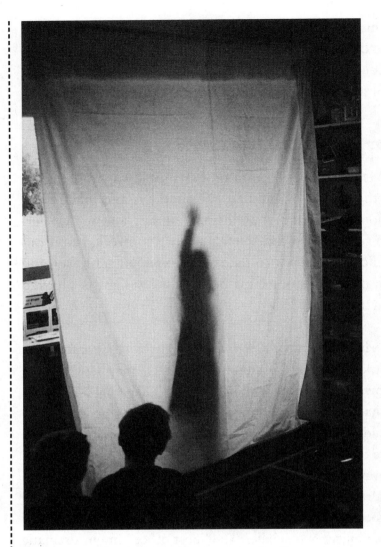

Figure 4–40 *Making Shadows on a Sheet*

They said things like: "You're making shadows." "Indoor shadows." "Shadow puppets." "Shadow plays." After our shadow play, I told the children that soon they could make their own shadow plays too, with puppets, their bodies, or just their hands. *Shadow Night* actually includes pictures showing how to hold your fingers just right to make different animals, from spiders to elephants to alligators to dogs to geese. I showed them the pictures and said I had copied some and would hang them up in the theater where they could see them and try them out.

For weeks, the kids explored shadows in different ways. I was very excited because I had not previously worked with a group that became so engaged. Some children were into making shadows with their entire bodies. As they stood close to the screen, their shadows became clear and distinct. Leaning backward, shadows grew big and fuzzy. "Look it's grow-ing!" shouted a child as she stretched her body high.

A friend stood wiggling his hand to cast a shadow. "A spider! It looks like a spider. My hand made a spider!" Quickly hands were twisted and shaped to create the images of recognizable animals. The children also began to recognize the silhouettes of friends: "I can tell that's Ben back there. His hair is curly." One child ran to her cubby, grabbed her winter hat, and stepped into the theater. Before her grew a shadow with two tas-sels perched on the top of her head. Meanwhile another child quietly formed shapes on the screen, softly talking to herself. When she was done she looked up at me and cheerfully said, "I just told a haunted hand story!"

Other children made their own puppets by pasting together colorful fabrics and paper samples to make simple cardboard body shapes. At first, the "puppet children" focused on their own puppets. Moving high and low on the screen, a child would say, "I can make it hop really high. Oops, it crashed!" Then the puppets began moving across the screen and, eventually, the puppets began to talk with one another. And the au-dience was delighted to discover that the colors of the puppets showed

Figure 4–41a *Shadow Puppet Plays*

through the screen. "Look, that one sparkles!" commented a child who was watching a puppet decorated with glossy purple paper.

The children definitely noticed the changes that were happening—shadows getting bigger or smaller or skinnier—but I wanted to help them share their thinking about *how* to change the shapes and sizes of shadows. So one afternoon, after they had been exploring shadows for a few weeks, I brought the whole group together around the shadow theater. "Time for today's shadow show," I told them. The children took turns making different shadows. Willie made a shadow goose. Costanza made an alligator. Ben made a monster. Then I asked them what they needed to do to make their shadows big. Andrew got up and walked away from the screen. "Can the rest of you show me?" I asked, and all the shadow kids moved farther away to make their creatures big. "Can you make them even bigger—into giants?" I asked. The children took giant steps backward. I asked them, "So what do you need to do to make your shadows small?" The children yelled out, "Move closer." The shadow kids moved close to the screen to make their shadows small. "Now can you make your shadows skinny?" The shadow kids experimented then, moving their hands up and down. Then Andrew turned his "monster hand" sideways and his monster shadow got skinny. "It's skinny," the audience called out. "You made it skinny." "How did you make it skinny?"

Figure 4–41b *Shadow Puppet Plays*

Figure 4–41c *Shadow Puppet Plays*

Figure 4–41d *Shadow Puppet Plays*

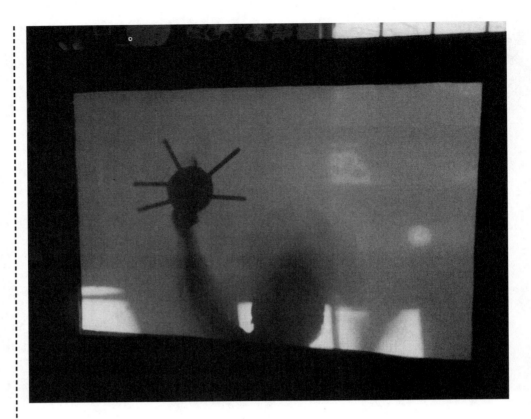

Figure 4–41e *Shadow Puppet Plays*

I asked. "Gotta turn it like this," Andrew said, demonstrating. "Oh," I said. "So you have to turn him sideways." As I recorded the children's ideas about how they could make their shadows big or small or skinny, it struck me that the children were really beginning to see the connections between cause and effect!

The study of shadows is not dependent on lots of materials or equipment, but does require a light source and a "screen" for the shadows. Ms. Tomas' first setup with the sheet and the natural light from the window helped the children transition their shadow play from outside to inside. The children could still use their whole bodies to make shadows, but now could see them in front of them rather than on the ground. The puppet theater, smaller and with an actual lamp, provided the opportunity and the motivation for the children to use smaller objects they had made, as well as their hands and parts of their bodies. The sharper shadows created by the lamps also encouraged more detailed work and a focus on what shadows each object would make. They also explored the relationship between an object's location and its shadow's size.

The use of both the sheet and the screen introduced the idea of theater or performance with an audience on the other side. Clearly, this provided the children with a playful context in which to create shadows and make them move and change. By spending weeks playing with hand shadows and puppets, the children had become very familiar with shadows. But Ms. Tomas realized that familiarity may not lead to deeper understanding. She, therefore, engaged the children in conversations and demonstrations focused on how to control the size and shape of the shadows by moving the objects. She also encouraged the children to theorize and test their theories. Not only did these conversations extend the children's thinking, they also provided Ms. Tomas with new insights into the children's thinking.

Shadow Corner: Opaque and Transparent

As the interest in shadows continued, Ms. Tomas decided to set up one more center where the children could explore shadows in another way. The overhead projector offered the opportunity to focus in on what one could and could not learn about an object from a shadow. As the story suggests, another concept emerged as the children were working: light can show through some objects!

Because the kids were so into shadows, I decided to set up a "shadow corner." There, I put an overhead projector on a table, shining it on a big pull-down screen. The four-year-olds were into making shadows. At first, they would stand in front of the screen, making shadows with their bodies and with their puppets. Then, Costanza put her puppet on top of the overhead and was surprised when she didn't see much on the paper screen. "Hey, I lost my shadow. What happened to my shadow?" (The puppet was big and covered much of the overhead screen. However, the image that shined on the screen was fuzzy.) "Let's try something else," said Andrew. So they put the puppets on the floor and tried putting plastic shapes on the overhead. This turned into a game of "guess what I'm putting on the overhead." A few of the three-year-olds in the class joined in and sat between the overhead projector and the pull-down screen. They were entranced as they watched the screen and tried to figure out what was making the shadow. "It's a donut!" "It's a lion!" "A T-rex!"

I noticed what was going on and talked with the group about their observations and about which things were easier than others to guess. A couple kids figured that the flatter the thing was, the easier it was to guess—like a puzzle piece or one of the flannel board shapes. But the pencil was easy, too, and it was round. I encouraged the children to draw pictures, showing what their shadows looked like on the overhead. I was amazed when the kids described their drawings, pointing out where the light came from.

The next day a child said, "Ms. Tomas, you gotta see this." One of the children had put a color paddle on the projector and there on the screen was the red paddle. "It's colored." I asked why they thought this made a colored shadow and the puzzle pieces didn't. I suggested they look for other things they thought might let the color through. This led to a lot of trial and error using different-colored things in the classroom. I didn't want them to get discouraged, so I offered one child our colored translucent counters. It worked and they were thrilled, trying them all out and seeing the colored disks on the screen. Then there were the soda bottles that one child brought in and some colored cellophane from someone else.

After this had gone on for a few days, I decided to get the children who had been part of this together to talk about what they had discovered. A couple of threes listened in, but I'm not sure how much they took away. The older ones were quite intrigued by the color. "Some things make a black shadow." "They're dark." "You can't see any color." "The colored things are shinier." "They look neat." At one point I felt that they would understand when I said that some light was shining through the objects and that when that happened we called the thing "translucent." Then I said that when the shadow was all black, there was no light shining and we called that "opaque." I didn't care whether they remembered the words but thought that a few might enjoy using them. After that discussion, a few of the children continued to look for things that would have a colored shadow.

The children in this class had played with the shadows created by the sun outdoors, those made on a sheet from the daylight coming in the window, and those created with a strong light source in their shadow puppet theater. The overhead projector was yet another way to create shadows that were sharp and crisp, and thus focused on the actual outline of objects. By engaging with shadows in a variety of ways, the children were able to build on their experiences, make connections between them, and develop new ideas.

The colored projections from the overhead took a group of children in an unplanned direction. Ms. Tomas' original focus was not on color or how much light went through the object. But given the children's interest, she followed up. She also had certainly not set out to teach the children the vocabulary words *translucent* and *opaque*. Direct teaching of vocabulary in science can leave children with words for which they have little underlying understanding, but modeling "big words" as children explore and describe the thing or event is important, and some children will enjoy using them.

Summing Up

The basic tasks of teaching science are described in Chapter One. But, just as in the life sciences, there are specific strategies that are particularly important for the study of physical science topics. Thinking back over the stories of Ms. Diego, Ms. Chin, Mr. Jacobson, and Ms. Tomas, the following are important similarities in how they planned, guided, and facilitated the children's explorations.

- All of the teachers chose a focus for inquiry and had specific concepts and ideas they wanted the children to experience and think about.

- Each teacher spent some time working with the materials themselves so they would have a better understanding of what might happen and how to support and guide the children in their work.

- In each of the stories, these teachers carefully constructed a physical environment that supported inquiry into the selected topic. This included a redesign of the working space to allow a good number of children to work in different spaces at the same time and to provide easy access to necessary materials.

- The teachers paid careful attention to the materials they made available. They added materials that would focus the children on the selected concepts and temporarily removed those that supported other kinds of work and play.

- All of the stories are about the exploration of materials that are also very conducive to sociodramatic play. There are many descriptions of how these teachers observed and acknowledged this play, while creating a science focus.

- Each teacher provided the children with opportunities to explore the topic in a variety of different ways, using different materials and working in different settings.

- In each story, there was a mix of open exploration, guided investigation, and challenges, which provided opportunities for the children to follow their own questions and focus on the specific science goals of the teacher.

- In each story, there were many examples of the children using evidence from their activity to construct theories and explanations for what was happening.

- As in the life science stories, the teachers used science talks and informal discussion to encourage the children to share and clarify their thinking and as a way to assess the children's understanding.

Earth and Space Science in the Early Childhood Classroom

In many ways earth and space science is the most complex of the sciences. To understand the structure of the earth and its history, climate, and meteorology, the solar system, and the universe requires understanding of many of the concepts of life and physical sciences. In addition, studying the ideas of earth and space science means thinking about long time scales, unseen forces, and faraway places. These complicated ideas including plate tectonics, the rock and water cycles, evolution, and the origins of the universe certainly do not belong in the early childhood curriculum.

However, children do come into direct contact with many aspects of earth and space science that they can explore and ponder. Wherever they live, there are earth materials to explore such as rocks, sand, and soil. Water is everywhere in streams, rivers, lakes, and oceans. Rain falls; puddles come and go; things get washed away. Young children experience the changes related to night and day, weather, and the seasons. And they can see the sun and the moon moving across the sky. Because of these daily experiences and interactions, earth and space science has a place in the early childhood classroom.

Doing Inquiry

The nature of inquiry in earth and space science depends a great deal on the topic. A study of the weather, the changing shape of the moon, or the movement of the sun across the sky requires systematic observation and recording of data. The daily weather chart, a familiar activity in early childhood classrooms, is a good example of systematic recording, and even young children can look for patterns in the data and changes over time.

A study of rocks requires close observation, comparison, and categorization, as does examination of different kinds of sand and soil. A closer look at water in the environment may lead to direct investigation of what happens when water is poured into a sand table or a little rivulet dams up on the playground.

Just as with life science, engaging in earth science can foster the beginnings of important attitudes and dispositions. As children become familiar with their environment and observe the changes taking place, they are likely to take notice and develop an appreciation for the world around them and their role in caring for it.

Engaging with Content

Through their experiences, children can think about earth materials in their environment, changes that occur around them (including weather, night and day, water on the playground), and patterns of movement and change of the sun and moon. These experiences provide children with a foundation for understanding more abstract concepts of earth systems, the history of the earth, and the earth's place in the solar system.

Much of the exploration of ideas and concepts from earth and space science is a natural extension of children's work in life and physical sciences. Earth materials might have been studied as an extension of Ms. Howard's and Miss Scott's work with animals and plants. Ms. Tomas' study of shadows might have led to observation of the movement of the sun.

We have divided the content of earth and space science into three parts that reflect young children's experiences: Properties of Earth Materials, Weather and Climate, and Patterns of Movement and Change of the Sun and the Moon. Each area includes a science explanation to suggest the level of understanding children may acquire, followed by examples of ways in which the content may be integrated across the curriculum.

Properties of Earth Materials

Young children are familiar with earth materials in their immediate environment and, in particular, the soil, sand, and rocks that are all around them. If they look more closely at these materials, they can see what their properties are and how they differ. They can observe what was found where, and wonder about how it might have gotten there. Through their experiences, children can begin to notice that soil is made up of different materials and that there are different kinds with different properties. By collecting and examining rocks, children begin to notice that they come in many shapes and sizes and have different colors and textures.

But the exploration of earth materials also can be part of other studies. For example, in Ms. Howard's story about worms, the question of where to find the little animals led to a closer look at the conditions in which they were found, including the earth materials (e.g., soil and rock). This might easily have led to a discussion of the nature of the particular location. "What kind of soil did the worms seem to prefer?" "Did the worms hide under the rocks?" The process of bringing in the worm visitors provided the opportunity to discuss what was needed to create a temporary home—soil! Ms. Howard might well have chosen to pursue the study of rocks and soil more deeply once the worms were in.

Water is an earth material as well and is critical to life on earth. In the story in this chapter, an exploration of water indoors leads to a focus on a nearby stream and some of the ways in which water plays a role on the earth's surface.

Weather and Climate

Recording the weather is a familiar activity in many classrooms. Going beyond this simple routine can provide children with the opportunity to think more about the weather and patterns of change. As data is collected and recorded on charts and graphs, children can discuss weather patterns and seasonal changes with questions such as "How many cloudy days did we have last week?" "How many rainy days have we had in September?" "When was the first snowfall?" "Did we have more sunny days this month than last?" "When did it start getting really cold?"

Children also can explore the impact of weather and seasons on themselves and the short- and long-term changes they can cause in the environment around them. They notice and can record immediate changes as the rain falls and the wind blows. They can question the appearance of puddles on the playground and can watch those puddles disappear or turn to ice as temperatures fall. And children can also become aware of slower changes, such as erosion on a hillside or gullies forming under rainspouts.

Weather may also be part of children's explorations in life and physical sciences. Teachers can highlight the role of weather as children explore living things in the environment. If rain doesn't reach the corner under the roof of the building, plants won't grow there. If there is too much rain, drowned worms appear on the sidewalk. When it begins to get cold they can no longer find bugs outdoors. And as children explore water, teachers can connect their work to the rain: how it falls, where it goes, how it moves.

Patterns of Movement and Change of the Sun and the Moon

Young children are certainly aware that the moon and the sun are in the sky and that they are not always in the same place. But they may not have noticed some of the more subtle changes. For instance, sometimes the moon can be seen at night, sometimes in the day. It changes shape over time from a full circle to different-size parts of a circle, and can look very big or quite small. The sun, on the other hand, is up during the day, moves across the sky, and disappears at night. As teachers encourage children to observe the moon and the sun more closely and help them to record their observations regularly, children can notice patterns of movement and change, and even make predictions about what they might see at different times.

As with previous earth and space science ideas, these can be highlighted as children explore other areas of science. When studying the living things outdoors or planting a garden, it is important to know how long the sun shines on a particular location, which may lead them to begin to notice how the sun shines on different areas at different times of the day, and that the amount of time changes at different times of the year. Ms. Tomas began her class' study of shadows outdoors and included drawing the children's shadows at different times of the day. After the class had taken their exploration of shadows indoors for a time, she might have decided to return to those shadows outdoors and focus the children's attention on the question of why they changed and the movement of the sun.

 with Mr. Jones -

Mr. Jones is a pre-K teacher in a public elementary school of 300 children. He has a class of nineteen three- and four-year-olds. There is a patch of woods along the back of the playground with a stream running through it. The following story shows how Mr. Jones moved from a study of water and its properties to an outdoor study where the children focused on water as an earth material. These investigations laid the foundation for a study that would invite the children to take a closer look at the impact of the flowing water and the role of water in changing the surface of the earth.

The River

For weeks, the children had explored moving water using basters, cups, syringes, and "tornado tubes." I wanted to build on their interest in the way water moves and take them outdoors to see water in an outdoor context, and how it flows and changes its direction when something gets in its way. So I planned a trip to a nearby river. It was quite small and there was no danger of anyone falling in. I asked my assistant and one parent volunteer to come along to help out to be sure that we didn't have too many wet feet.

Before the trip, I prepared the children during a large-group discussion. First, we talked about how they used the different materials to move the water up or down or to make it stop. I asked Robin to demonstrate how she held the tube to make the water come out fast and then slowly. I told them that they had learned a lot about water. Now they were going to learn even more by going to the river and, using all their senses, see how the water feels, watch how it moves, and listen to how it sounds.

When we first got to the river, we observed some small rapids. I had the children sit near the edge and describe how the water moved. Ezra said that the water was moving all bumpy and kind of straight but it turned a corner too. Lynn had trouble finding the words to express what she had observed, so I asked her to show me with her body, and others joined in as well. They moved fast, taking quick little steps. Once in a while they would fall on the ground and roll forward to show the movement of the water over the rocks.

Then I told them they were going to close their eyes and listen to the water really, really carefully. They shut their eyes and listened. Then they described how the water sounded. Gabi said, "It sounds like my mom cooking a hamburger." Chris said, "It sounds like the water filling up my bathtub." Lynn said, "It sounds like my mother's washing machine." Nicholas said, "It sounds like the rain falling when I wake up and hear it." Terry said, "It is loud!" When I asked why, she said it was "because the water goes so fast!"

I then let the children go near the edge of the river and feel the movement of the water. Lynn said that the water ran down her arm and it felt "tickly." Gabi said the water pushed her hand. I asked her if she could push it back and she tried. "How does it feel to push it?" I asked. Gabi said, "It feels swishy. See, my hand moves from side to side and then up and down. It's swishy. Rubby swishy, like the water is rubbing my hand." Nicholas laughed, "My water is all crazy!" "What kind of crazy?" I asked him. He said, "It's spinning in circles this way and then the other way and rolly rolly."

Children's senses are their primary tools for inquiry. Teachers and children alike often rely only on sight; other senses are often neglected. The beginning of this story highlights how skillful teachers can help children use different senses to observe their environment and describe what they observe using interesting vocabulary.

The Stream

We began to walk alongside the water when the children discovered the much smaller stream that led into the river. It was about twelve inches deep at the deepest point. At first we talked about how the water moved. In low-flowing areas, the water moved slowly. In other areas, the water moved fast over and around rocks and tree branches. I wondered out loud why the water moved. Ezra said, "Maybe someone was pushing it, a motor somewhere." Lynn said, "Maybe it's a flat waterfall." I asked if a waterfall is flat, how can the water fall? They looked puzzled.

So we did an experiment. I had a clipboard with me and we found some sand at the edge of the little stream. "Pretend the sand is water," I said and put some on the clipboard: it didn't move. "I wonder why it didn't move," I said. Christian said it was because the board is flat. I said, "And if I tip the board up a little, will the sand roll?" They all said "yes." Then I propped the board up just a little and the sand started to slide down it. "What happened?" I asked. Everyone piped in, "It moved!" "Why?" I asked. Gabi said, " 'Cause it slided down the hill on the board." I responded, "Oh, so it needed a hill even if it's just a tiny hill. What about the streams—are they on hills too?" Gabi said, "Yeah, but you can't see it." Christian added, " 'Cause it's a really small hill." Lynn said, "But I can see it 'cause my eyes are strong."

For a while, the children watched as the water gushed through, over, and around the many obstacles in its way. I asked them what they noticed

Our Stream Trip

The water is very cold.

The rapids move because the water is on a hill.

You can't see the hill. It is too small.

The water makes noise because it bumps into things. It bumped into rocks and trees and logs.

We stopped the water by blocking it. That only worked for a little while because the water was too strong so the dam broke.

Figure 5–1

about what the water was doing. Christian said that the water "kind of goes underneath where the big waves are." Joanne said, "It looks bumpy and crazy when it moves." I asked why the water looked bumpy and crazy. Nicholas said, "'Cause someone put a lot of rocks in the way." I asked, "But why do the rocks make the water bumpy?" Gabi said it was because the water bumps into the rocks. After this conversation I asked them if there might be a way to stop the water from moving in the little stream. They said that we had to block it with big rocks. "Let's try it," said Gabi, so they began to find rocks and sticks and even small logs that they talked me into dragging over, and they successfully blocked the water flow. We watched for a while until the water began to fill up and then overflow the dam. They tried to build it higher but couldn't get it high enough to contain the water and the water eventually began to flow from around the sides.

The next day the children talked about their experiences. I made a chart to record their ideas.

Next week we'll start exploring erosion by experimenting with how water affects different materials, from piles of dirt to sand to rocks and ice.

Mr. Jones "wondered out loud" about why the water moved. With his question, Mr. Jones modeled wonder and curiosity. A comment, made this way, encourages children to speculate. In this case, they seemed to be making some connections to their thinking from the water explorations as they wondered about why the water might move. Mr. Jones' explanation using the sand on a sloping surface was unlikely to lead the children to an understanding of water and how it flows, but it gave the children something to think about, which they remembered the next day. And it was something to build on as they continued their investigation of water outdoors.

A Final Word

The study of earth and space science poses interesting challenges. Many of the concepts are very theoretical and the phenomena distant in time and space. Yet, at the same time, young children come to early childhood programs with many ideas and images from books and the media about space, dinosaurs, the formation of the earth, natural disasters such as volcanoes or earthquakes, and places that are very different from where they live. These topics are exciting and lead to imaginative talk and play. Children may even have interesting "theories" to explain what happened to the dinosaurs or what is in space. These ideas, as most ideas that capture children's imaginations, have a place in the classroom and can stimulate interesting thinking and activity.

Teachers can build on children's interests in topics such as space and dinosaurs through discussion, books, and toys. But as children share and discuss their early theories, it is important that teachers probe for their thinking but not impose scientifically accurate explanations (e.g., the earth moves around the sun; the seasons are caused by the tilt of the earth; the moon goes around the earth) before children's own experiences and level of thought enable them to grasp these concepts. We also do not recommend focused studies of the solar system, space, the formation of the earth, dinosaurs and fossils, or distant environments such as the rain forest for the early childhood science curriculum. Rather, the focus should be children's explorations of their immediate environment, where they can have direct experience with materials and events.

PART THREE

Final Words

CHAPTER 6

Questions and Thoughts

In this final chapter, we respond to some of the questions that practitioners raise about science teaching and learning in the early childhood classroom. We hope that our responses (not answers) will stimulate thoughtful discussion about ways to integrate science in the early childhood curriculum.

How is this different from the science the children and I are already doing?

In some classrooms, teachers set up a science table with interesting collections, such as shells and sea glass; magnifiers may invite closer observation; and related books and posters may be displayed. In other classrooms, teachers may implement theme-based curricula, focusing on such topics as bears or apples. And in still other classrooms, science may be a weekly activity—magnets one week and blowing bubbles the next. What is missing from all of these approaches is a serious emphasis on critical elements of children's scientific inquiry, appropriate science content goals, and opportunities for children to pursue their own questions and interests in depth over time.

Children do explore interesting science-related materials in everyday classroom activities as they play with blocks, sand, and water, but teachers rarely use these as opportunities to focus on the science. As Mr. Jacobson said, for years he rarely engaged with the children in the block area. He viewed the block area as a place for the children's dramatic play and spontaneous work. But he learned that the block area could also be a place for science teaching and learning. That is, while the block area could engage the children in building a house for their bear to live in, he could also use their experiences to help them explore balance and forces.

Is subject matter really important as long as children learn science inquiry skills?

Yes. This question of content versus process has been debated for many years. In this book we have argued that both are important. The skills of inquiry—from observing to using tools to designing investigations to constructing theories—are fundamental to learning science and important in many areas of early childhood learning. In fact, many of these skills are identified as important objectives for the early childhood classroom. But these skills need to be learned and practiced. Choosing meaningful science content for children's inquiry is also important so that children can build a foundation for later deeper understanding of basic science concepts.

So, inquiry and subject matter are both important and cannot be separated. Children may need direct instruction for some specific skills, such as learning to use a magnifier. And they can practice some skills on their own, such as categorization. But children develop their inquiry skills as they investigate interesting subject matter, and children build theories about interesting subject matter through the use of inquiry skills.

What basic ideas in science should I cover?

In this book, we describe a set of basic science concepts in life, physical, and earth and space sciences that young children can inquire about through direct experience. Our purpose is to help teachers think about and select opportunities for children's inquiry instruction—not to identify specific outcomes for children's learning. Each set of concepts can be addressed through many topics, depending on the location, resources, and interests of the children and the teacher. For example, Ms. Chin's study of the motion of objects was based on her children's interests in building speedways and ramps for their trucks and cars; others might have chosen to embed this science in an exploration of toys.

It is not our expectation that teachers cover all of the science concepts in this book. Rather, what is important is for teachers to select a few concepts for children to explore in depth. Only by having multiple experiences with a few basic concepts can children make generalizations, draw conclusions, and construct new theories about the world around them. Two or three studies, such as those described by the teachers in this book, may well last throughout the year.

Can preschool children really do science?

This question is asked in a number of different contexts. Sometimes it is about whether children can really go beyond direct exploration to analyze their observations and reflect on their ideas and experiences. The examples in this book show that they can. To be sure, there are differences in what can be expected of three-year-old children compared with five-year-old children. But given direct experience with materials and thoughtful facilitation from adults, all children can build new ideas and refine their theories about how the world works.

Just as teachers ask if children are capable of analysis and reflection, others question if young children can record their work or participate in group discussions—two important elements in teaching and learning science. The examples of the children's work in this book provide a sense for the kinds of representation and recording children can do. In a classroom where dialogue about work and ideas is ongoing and interest in the science experiences is high, even groups of very young children can develop the skills to share, discuss, and listen.

Sometimes this question is asked about children with diverse needs. As with any subject area, the teacher must be a close observer of the children and open to their diverse strengths, challenges, interests, and perspectives. All children are building on their experiences to continuously try to make sense of their world. They all bring their experiences and theories to their work in the classroom. Good science materials are open-ended and accessible to children at many levels and with different experiences and backgrounds. All children can approach water play, the search for living organisms, or making shadows in their own way. When teachers observe children's play and work carefully, they can support and guide children on their own pathways.

Ultimately this question is about expectations. Both research and experience suggest that the expectations for what young children can do are often too low. The stories in this book and research findings, as well as experience in many classrooms, provide ample evidence that we must raise those expectations to encompass what children really can do when given the opportunity to engage deeply with science.

What is the role of child-initiated activity in science?

Teachers need to take a number of steps to create an environment to promote children's inquiry into a topic. They design the physical setting; they plan the areas of science they will focus on; they establish a set of overall goals. But once the environment is in place, children's explorations lead them in many directions—and many ideas, questions, and challenges arise. What actually happens emerges from a dynamic interaction among the children's interests and questions, the materials, and the teachers' goals for the children. For example, Ms. Diego chose a study of water and water flow, but as the children explored with the tubes and funnels, they became intrigued with air. In response, Ms. Diego added rigid tubes and pumps to the water table so the children could focus on the relationship between air and water.

What is the role of children's play in science?

Children's science is about play: play with materials and objects and events. We have found it very helpful to think about three kinds of play: dramatic play, exploratory play, and constructive play (Eisenberg 2000). Children can learn about science through dramatic play, particularly when teachers interact with them, gently focusing on the science that is inherent in their play. For example, in Ms. Diego's room, Pilar added a magic ingredient to her soup, using tubes and funnels and containers at the water table. Ms. Diego used this as an opportunity to focus Pilar's attention on water flow, asking her to demonstrate how she could control the amount of magic ingredient that went into the soup.

Exploratory play is about finding out. When it is focused on materials and events—trying to find out how to make something happen—it is very much about science. In this case, teachers support, guide, and challenge children to pursue their questions and ideas and focus on new ones. Some of the children in Ms. Diego's class wanted to use the interesting materials she had given them to explore what water did and how they could control it. And Ms. Chin's group took on the challenge of figuring out the relationship between the slope of the ramp and how far the balls would go.

And finally, in constructive play, science and technology come together as children take on the challenge of making something. A good example is the tower building in Mr. Jacobson's class: the children became deeply engaged in figuring out how high they could make their towers using different kinds of blocks.

How can science be added to the curriculum when the goals are focused on the development of literacy, math, and social skills?

Science is an important part of children's experience in school and should be valued in and of itself. It supports children's curiosity and their need to understand the world around them. Science is a natural focus for their work and play. But there need not be competition between devoting time to science and devoting time to the development of language, math, and social skills. As is evident in the stories and the children's work in this book, good science can permeate the classroom, providing the context for learning and practicing many skills. Science is about literacy. Children record their discoveries and observations; they talk about their work; they use new vocabulary; they use books to find things out. Science is also about mathematics. Children measure and count as they record data; they make charts and graphs from their data; they look for patterns and relationships in what they have observed. And science is about social skills as children work together with materials, share their ideas, and listen to the ideas of others. At the same time, children learn about themselves and their world.

How much science does the teacher need to know?

A solid background in science is not essential. But teachers do need to have a willingness to roll up their sleeves—to become inquirers, to play with the materials the children will be using, and to see and experience the phenomena themselves. They also need to begin to learn about the science through good books and other media resources that provide a beginning description of the different areas of science identified in the content chapters. Science resources for young people can also be very informative.

This knowledge and experience will help teachers make decisions about the design of the physical and social environment for exploration in their classrooms. It will help them to think about what children might be asking as they explore the materials. And it can inform decisions about the next steps for individuals and groups.

Many teachers worry that they will not be able to answer all the questions children will raise. This is probably true, but answering questions is not the teachers' role. Rather than providing answers, teachers should use children's questions as a springboard for further investigation. For example, teachers might say, "I don't know. Let's see if we can find out." Finding out might involve exploring further, reading a book, inviting a guest expert—which can lead to new discoveries, new questions, and new investigations.

These are just a few of the questions to think about when bringing real science inquiry into the early childhood curriculum. But what is most important is simply to get started. As the children begin to explore materials and ideas, their interest and excitement will be obvious and their activity will point the way to deeper and broader investigation. And as teachers observe and interact with children doing science, they will see for themselves what young children can really do and learn when science becomes a central focus of the early childhood curriculum.

WORKS CITED AND OTHER PROFESSIONAL PUBLICATIONS

American Association for the Advancement of Science. 1993. *Benchmarks for Science Literacy*. New York: Oxford University Press.

American Association for the Advancement of Science. 1999. *Dialogue on Early Childhood Science, Mathematics, and Technology Education*. Washington, DC: American Association for the Advancement of Science.

Bowman, Barbara T., M. Suzanne Donovan, and M. Susan Burns, eds. 2001. *Eager to Learn: Educating Our Preschoolers*. Washington, DC: National Academy Press.

Bransford, John D., Ann L. Brown, and Rodney R. Cocking, eds. 1999. *How People Learn: Brain, Mind, Experience, and School*. Washington, DC: National Academy Press.

Bredekamp, Sue, and Carol Copple, eds. 1997. *Developmentally Appropriate Practice in Early Childhood Programs* (revised ed.). Washington, DC: NAEYC.

Donovan, M. Suzanne, John D. Bransford, and James W. Pellegrino, eds. 1999. *How People Learn: Bridging Research and Practice*. Washington, DC: National Academy Press.

Eisenberg, Mary. 2000. *The Influence of Materials on Children's Play: Explorations at the Water Table*. Unpublished study, Tufts University.

National Research Council. 1996. *National Science Education Standards*. Washington, DC: National Academy Press.

Shonkoff, Jack P., and Deborah A. Phillips, eds. 2000. *From Neurons to Neighborhoods: The Science of Early Childhood Development*. Washington, DC: National Academy Press.

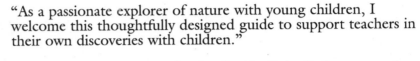
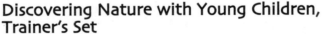